HOME BUSINESS SUCCESS SECRETS

5 Steps To Building An Automated Passive Income Stream Through The Unlimited Power Of Internet And Network Marketing

SIMON LEUNG

**WITH CONTRIBUTIONS FROM
20 SUCCESS STORIES SHARING THEIR
MOST EFFECTIVE STRATEGIES**

Home Business Success Secrets

Copyright © 2017 by Simon Leung. All Rights Reserved Worldwide.

No part of this book may be reproduced or transmitted in any form or by any means, electronic or mechanical, including photocopying, recording, or by an information storage and retrieval system - except by a reviewer who may quote brief passages in a review to be printed in a magazine or newspaper - without permission in writing from Simon Leung (the "Author").

For information contact:
http://www.simonleung.com

ISBN-13: 978-1543200812
ISBN-10: 1543200818
First Edition: January 2017
10 9 8 7 6 5 4 3 2 1

WHY THIS BOOK HAS BEEN CALLED A "MUST-READ" RESOURCE FOR ALL HOME BUSINESS ENTREPRENEURS

(MORE TEAM MEMBER TESTIMONIALS TOWARDS THE END OF THE BOOK)

*****

"Howdy y'all! I just got to know Simon Leung only 48 hours ago, and he has already helped increase subscribers to my home business v-blog by 10 (ten) folds. His online marketing strategies are amazing!" – Dewi Kurniawati

"Being new in this Internet and network marketing business, the journey was not easy for me but I'm very grateful and honor that I have met my mentor, Simon Leung. Under his mentorship and guidance, I managed to apply what I have learnt from him and able to earn USD by following his step by steps. Choosing the right mentor is very important to be success in Internet and network marketing business. I have chosen mine, have you chosen yours?" – Hui Min

"I never knew that I could earn USD online so easily until I met Simon Leung. Under his mentorship and guidance, I managed to learn valuable skills and knowledge in home business. I am so grateful that he and his team have helped me to achieve my financial freedom." – Leow Yin Chi

"Internet Marketing is a powerful and effective skill to boost up sales in today's marketplace. I have started to believe it is possible to generate sales from nowhere. It's an awesome experience and pleasure to have a great mentor like Simon Leung and his Protégés to guide and support us towards the success path." – Chong Ming

"I came across this opportunity to learn Internet marketing from Simon Leung and his amazing team of mentors. This has opened up my eyes and changed my perspective on the way online business works. These skills are helpful for anyone who would like to venture into home business and Internet marketing." – Hwooi Foo

"After joining Simon Leung's Internet & network marketing business, I have learnt so many skills that are outside of my knowledge. His mentoring added value not just in business, but also personal improvement. I'm forever grateful to him and his team for adding value in my life." – Chilli Yong

"I'm so lucky to have the rare opportunity to partner with my mentor, Simon Leung, and his Protégés, working together towards a common goal. Without any employees, it's still possible to build your ecommerce business right from home. It's great to step in this business to make USD online, with their guidance and proven Online Marketing System, I believe everyone is able to step in to build their own Internet Empire World." – Nicholas Lau Seng Wan

ACKNOWLEDGEMENTS

*****

To my family, who has always been supportive and the true inspiration behind all my hard work and subsequent creation of this book. You are the reason I have and always will continue to strive to be the best that I can be.

To my good friends and business partners, who introduced me to the business and the reasons for my achievements in this industry today. Thank you for taking me by the hand and teaching me how to lead and follow the right way.

To my mentor in this business, who has graciously agreed to provide masterpiece value by contributing to the Foreword of this book. Your contribution means so much more than you can ever imagine, and I can't wait to see how many more lives we will be able to touch because of you.

To my Protégé Team, who truly embraced the opportunity to become entrepreneurs and Lead Mentors for our team members. Without you, we would not have led so many to the top of the mountain. Your effort to lead, train and support the team is the reason we have successfully continued to build more and more successes around the world.

To my book contributors and featured testimonials, who blindly accepted a random writing project with no promise of fame or fortune in the notion of sharing value through your own personal experiences to help people you don't even know. Consisting of my team leaders and elite members, you have earned this opportunity and I want to congratulate you for stepping up and carrying the weight of leading a team towards your imminent success.

To you, who have made the commitment to enrich yourself by taking the time to read this book. You truly humble and encourage me to continue my journey to make this world a better place through my online and offline educational efforts.

I am blessed to have all of you in my life. You inspire me every morning to be a better person, to strive towards greater and higher heights, and I appreciate you for that. Thank you!

TABLE OF CONTENTS

*****

PREFACE
Do You Belong Here?..1

FOREWORD BY BILLY TEOH
Founder Of ACES Worldwide
The Double Diamond Director's Simple Secret To Network Marketing Success...5

INTRODUCTION
The Best Of Both Worlds...15

CHAPTER ONE
Why Are You Reading This Book?......................................21

CHAPTER TWO
How To Collect Unlimited Names And Contact Details Online Like Virtual Business Cards.......................................47

CHAPTER THREE
This Is What You Will Be Doing Online All Day Long......73

TABLE OF CONTENTS (PART 2)

*****

CHAPTER FOUR
Build Your Business... By Giving Away Free Gifts!............99

CHAPTER FIVE
Introduce The Business Opportunity For The First Time...123

CHAPTER SIX
If At First You Don't Succeed…...149

CHAPTER SEVEN
Lead Your Team To Network Marketing Success..............177

CHAPTER EIGHT
Automating The Entire Process To Help You Sign Up New Partners From "Out Of Nowhere".......................................197

CONCLUSION
Ready To Take Massive Action?..223

TABLE OF CONTENTS (PART 3)

*****

AFTERWORD BY JERRY CHEN WITH MICHAEL SINGLETON (DIAMOND LEADERS)
Special Bonus Chapter – Putting It All Together: The Diamond Leader's Favorite Private Method To Personally Sponsoring, Maintaining And Motivating Over 2,800 Global Partners And Customers.................................227

RESOURCES
Access Free Gifts, Surprise Bonuses & Live Demos Of Our Online Systems In Action..257

TESTIMONIALS
What More Team Members Say About The Strategies Outlined In This Book...259

ABOUT THE AUTHOR..263

MEET THE CONTRIBUTORS....................................265

PREFACE
Do You Belong Here?
*****

Entrepreneurship is something many people dream about, but the vast majority of the world's population will almost never get around to it. Why is that?

To most aspiring entrepreneurs, building their own business from the ground up often means investments, skills and a whole lot of work, all of which they do not have the time or resources to attain. Unfortunately, this also means putting their own objectives on hold.

Then, there are those who dare to challenge the norm. These are the ones who do not necessarily go after creating their own products or services, but have figured out a way to truly leverage on existing commodities to branch themselves to new levels.

These are the entrepreneurs who understand the

value of learning, teamwork, and continued perseverance. It is because of this open-minded understanding that they are able to take existing business models and revolutionize their success with the use of state-of-the-art and automated online technology.

What it really boils down to is an individual's ability to see past the negative noises that exist both internally and externally, and recognize that when provided with the right system and mentorship, anybody can be successful in whatever venture they wish to chase.

If this accurately describes you, then you have come to the right place. We are here today not to talk about simply any kind of entrepreneurship, but a rather unique one.

What if I were to tell you that it is not a requirement to have your own product or service to start a profitable business? What if you discovered a way to begin a new venture without even five or six figures worth of financial investment? How about that it is possible for you to jump right in even if you do not have any relevant experience whatsoever?

Yes, it exists, and chances are, you have already heard of it. It is called a home-based business, and there is a wide variety from which you can choose.

The most popular ones, which have created the

most successes, are undoubtedly network marketing and online marketing. Individually, each has the potential to make anyone a good living. Together, on the other hand, they can give you successes beyond your wildest imagination.

In this book, we are not going to explain too deeply into the definitions of network marketing and online marketing, or the history of these two industries. If you what to learn more about them, a quick Google search will give you the answers you need.

Rather, we are going to dive right into how you can combine the two of them to truly transform a simple home-based business into a 24/7 passive income-generating machine.

Keep in mind that while this may be one of the fastest and easiest home businesses to start up, is also not for the faint of heart or those who tend to give up easily. Still here? Good, let's begin.

Home Business Success Secrets

FOREWORD BY BILLY TEOH
Founder Of ACES Worldwide
"The Double Diamond Director's Simple Secret To Network Marketing Success"

*****

My name is Billy Teoh, and I am the Founder of ACES Worldwide. At ACES, our mission is to educate passionate people around the world about health and wellness. It's because of this simple yet effective concept that I was able to become my company's first and only Double Diamond Director in both Singapore and Malaysia.

Many people want to know the secret to network marketing success. Whether from the industry's reputation to individual skill sets, countless challenges await each and everyone in direct sales. Success is the journey of overcoming all these challenges.

Overcoming challenges is not an easy task. It requires skills, discipline and the consistent learning of new things. Is it worth it? Is MLM really that good?

Well, it depends who you are and how you do things differently. The same rule applies if you were to ask if a knife is a good or bad thing. It depends on who is holding the knife in the first place.

If it's a doctor, it will save lives. If it's an artist, it will create a masterpiece. If it's a chef, it will prepare delicious food. If it's a child, it may cut them. If it's a robber, it can cut others.

Likewise, MLM can be good or bad depending on who's taking charge. There's no doubt that the money is good, but if it gets in the hands of someone who doesn't know what they're doing or potentially possesses bad intentions, the end result can be as dangerous as a knife held by a robber.

Everyone's success rate is different because everyone has a different set of skills, background and personal level of commitment. However, based on my own experience, I can say that the chances of success are much higher when you combine online with offline, led by experienced gurus to guide the way.

For me, I built my business mostly the tradition way with years of hard work. I started by talking to people one by one, and let me tell you, I've had many cups of coffee and tea while meeting with all kinds of people in the process of building my business.

Although in this day and age of technology, I saw the potential of doing all this traditional hard work online, and we have grown exponentially since taking the business onto the Internet. I have even witnessed with my own two eyes the impact of the online world, and can say that for those who recently joined this business, it has now become all about the Internet.

What's so beautiful about the Internet?

Online, new partners can sign up without your presence or even direct attention. You don't have to make presentations or deliver on anything. There are no logistics, storage or anything to worry about. Even when you're sleeping, people are ordering online. The Internet is the only way to do this.

This is revolutionary for people who see network marketing as a hard business, and so they want to search for solutions to make it easy. When you find yourself at the crossroads and must choose between the hard way or the easy way, I say choose the right way.

Nothing in life is easy. Everything has obstacles. The difference is that for this business, you only need to work hard once. I worked hard for four years before achieving my current level of success. Confronting your challenges head on is the only way to break through all the barriers.

When you approach this business traditionally by talking to people, it doesn't necessarily need to be difficult. Similarly, when you approach this business unconventionally by doing it online or even with a proven model, it doesn't guarantee that it would be simple. That's why neither can be classified to be the correct way, at least not in my book.

Then, what is the right way?

Before we talk about the right way, let's talk about the wrong way. Personally, I don't like to sell, and I also don't like to be sold. Whenever people I know approach me about a new business opportunity, I tell them to stop right there in their tracks, as I would prefer to maintain our friendship.

For a long time, I was not opened to the idea of network marketing, and I never considered it until someone helped me to clear my doubts by evaluating the pros and cons of the business.

I soon realized that it wasn't the business model I disliked. In fact, the business model is superb, and there are millions waiting to be made. What I didn't like about the industry was how most people operated in their quests to build the business.

Yes, there are many people who want to take the easy way out, and in the process, do everything completely wrong. They approach their family and friends, attempt to sell them on all the benefits of the company and products, and unfortunately, become so aggressive that they affect relationships in the process.

This person convinced me that there is a right way to do this, a less invasive way and much more effective method that would not spoil any existing relationships, but rather, make them even better. The right way is simply to share.

When products are good, they touch lives. I believe in my company's products and have full confidence that the cutting edge technology behind them has the power to change lives forever.

This science has literally saved lives, and when I share real life-changing results, I don't need to sell. The products speak for themselves, and I would be doing my contacts a disfavor if I don't share this with them.

Yet, not everyone can do it. Many are still struggling to make the system work for them. It's as easy as summoning the courage to open your mouth and share. What's so difficult about that?

You know it's a funny world when everyone is given the exact same system, yet some make it to a huge success while others fail miserably. The reason is simple. Those who fail simply do not respect the system and the rule of the game.

If you visit a new country, you need to know which side of the street to traffic flows. If you go hiking, you need to be equipped with the right shoes, tools and appropriate apparatus. One mishap can have disastrous consequences.

In this business, you need to have the same approach. There are things you need to do, practice, and prepare. Don't look for shortcuts as there's no such thing as hard or easy, only a matter of doing it right or wrong. When you learn how to do it the right way, you're then ready to step up to the next level towards success, and that is to become the right leader.

The right leader knows, understands and applies true leadership. True leaders understand the importance of the system that is replicable. They trust it and follow it. However, true leadership is much deeper than that.

What makes a true leader?

Firstly, become a leader yourself. Leaders always have followers. Secondly, develop more leaders from those followers. They will pave the way to create additional leaders. Finally, ensure the unity of all the leaders by unifying the leadership team.

Once you become a true leader, you then need to realize that it's not only about you. It has never been only about you. The power comes in numbers, and once you are cohesive as a team, doing the same things together, you become unstoppable.

When Michael Jackson performed his dance moves, it may be awkward to some if he was dancing alone and drew attention to certain parts of his body. However, when the King of Pop did the same moves with a group of dancers and they all performed it together, the result was a magical dance experience.

This is what I mean by system. A system that is created to work by a leader would make it replicable by the followers around them. They then become the next leaders, and the process continues from there.

Always teach and encourage the duplication of the system, and while it can always be improved, don't reinvent it. Systems work. Don't change what works.

When you finally realize that it's not about you and how you can achieve certain ranks, qualifications or goals, but rather how you can help your fellow team members achieve them, it will suddenly become a totally different ballgame. You will feel less pressure and burden, and at the same time, you will be more motivated because you know you're working towards helping each other attain a common victory.

Believe that you're here for a reason. Trust that your goal is to help as many people as you can. Educate anyone who would listen about the products, speak of the benefits and share real testimonials of those in the same situations as them.

To do this, you must be attentive. Have the passion and attitude of always wanting to help other people, and know that through you, their lives can change for the better. Don't be afraid to talk to them. If you are afraid to talk to people, then people will be afraid to talk to you. Nobody wins.

Don't waste anymore time. Overcome your own fears, jump straight in and just do it. If not now, when? If this is not a good opportunity, what is? If you do not do it, who will?

Even if you are normally a cool person, be crazy just this once. Don't lose your chance to change lives globally, while making a huge difference in your own in the process.

At the end day, know with absolute certainty what you want, and stop at nothing to achieve it. As long as you do it with integrity and righteousness, I don't see anything capable of standing in your way.

If you need to learn, learn from the best. Be willing to invest in the very best so you can also become your best. The good news is that you have one of the very best in your hands right now.

Don't let anyone tell you that you can't do it. Those who tell you that do so because they can't do it themselves. Don't allow yourself to be judged or influenced by others. Continue moving forward for yourself and your family, and nobody else.

In closing, while you must milk every drop of learning possible from this book and apply what is applicable to you, do not hold this as the Bible. As entrepreneurs destined for bigger and greater success, we must continue to grow as necessary.

Trends will change, times will change, and people will change. Prepare to read the next book, prepare to improve throughout the journey, and prepare to become a better person along the way. This is what your life is all about.

If you are prepared to be a success, and prepared to change lives in addition to your own, then ACES Worldwide welcomes you with open arms. At ACES, we invite you to partake in our extremely worthwhile global mission of educating passionate people around the world about health and wellness.

Not only that, but we enjoy many company incentive trips to places like Dubai, Orlando, Europe and the Mediterranean cruise, just to name a few. It's not so much about the trips themselves since anyone with money can go.

However, what if the trips are free? What if your whole team can all go at the same time? I'll tell you, nothing is more exhilarating than achieving the same goals together as a team.

My secret for success is simple. If you're going to learn, learn from the best. If you're going to do, do it for the best. In all my years of network marketing experience, I can tell you with full confidence that this is the best, and you now have the chance to be a part of it, along with the formula to do it all online.

Congratulations on your decision to educate yourself, and I eagerly anticipate hearing about your imminent success!

Billy Teoh
Founder of ACES Worldwide

INTRODUCTION
The Best Of Both Worlds
*****

When it comes to home business entrepreneurship, the two prominent success stories have always come from either network marketers or Internet marketers.

Strangely enough, it is usually these two same industries that often receive the most backlash from the business communities. Whenever there is a new opportunity, most people would be excited to learn more about it or may even be eager to potentially join, only to back out once it is revealed that the project itself is a network marketing or Internet marketing business.

Perhaps it is because society has done such a good job programming the population about what is to be expected when running a business. Ever since the beginning of time, we were taught to study hard in school so we can learn the skills to land a good job.

Then, we are to work in this job for years, maybe decades, in order to save up for a "real" business that requires huge financial investments towards products, services, employees, physical stores and other necessities.

It does not occur to most aspiring entrepreneurs that time has changed. No longer are any of the aforementioned business investments necessary. In fact, it is now perfectly plausible for anyone to start a new business with zero experience, small investment and almost no overhead.

This is the beauty of having your own network marketing or Internet marketing business. However, contrary to popular belief, it is not one or the other.

I personally stumbled upon this amazing combination completely by accident while networking at one of the many seminars where I was a featured speaker.

As a speaker, it is not uncommon for me to be approached by attendees who would subsequently propose potential projects we could work on together. At one particular event, I was given a proposal to join a network marketing company.

My initial reaction was that I had no interest. After all, I was familiar with network marketing, and while I know it to be an extremely profitable business model for those who had the skills and personality, as an introvert, I felt that it was not for me.

When the attendee later introduced himself as a co-founder of the company and their vision to promote the business online, that was when a light bulb went off in my head.

"Why didn't I think of that?" I thought to myself. With the lucrative possibilities in network marketing combined with the power of Internet marketing platforms and automation tools, this is literally putting together the best of both worlds.

Imagine receiving the same commission checks as those who spent years growing their businesses and are now making millions, except unlike them, you do not need to talk to your friends or family members, make any personal presentations whatsoever, or even have to speak to anyone at all.

I mean, I had been making money online for years without talking to anybody or even knowing the identity of my customers. Why can't we do the same thing for network marketing?

The answer: We most definitely can, and with very little effort, we proved it.

This particular network marketing company was giving away free BMWs at the time to top performers who had hit a certain level. The record for the fastest BMW earner back then was 7 days from an experienced network marketer who bent over backwards hustling to break the previous record of 30 days.

As you can imagine, smashing a record like this was no easy task, as earning a prestigious brand new BMW would definitely not be easy. Even with all those years of experience, it took this particular network marketer an entire week of long meetings, presenting and even calling in favors in order to achieve the prize. However, after launching my online campaign, I qualified for my free BMW in less than 24 hours – without even breaking a sweat.

After so many years of avoiding network marketing like a plague, I had finally cracked the code to making it profitable for somebody like me who loathed personal selling with a passion. The secret was under my nose the entire time: Simply do it online.

As an Internet entrepreneur who has been programmed with achieving success through multiple sources of income, my online network marketing journey did not stop there.

In addition to continuing my usual businesses, I also tested this system further on more network marketing companies. The result? They have all proven to become successful from just 5 simple steps.

With these online strategies, I managed to hit major ranks, achieved contest prizes and even recognized on stage for my accomplishments. The funny thing was that I did not know or even talked to my new members prior to them signing up online.

That's not even the most beautiful part. As an Internet marketing trainer and speaker, my focus has always been to make successes out of ordinary people. That's why I travel around the world and speak across dozens of countries and cities a year.

Because network marketing is a business with existing quality products and services, this makes it so much easier to plug anyone into the business while implementing the online strategies I had been using to build my own network.

When all is said and done, the most beautiful part is that success with this system is easily replicated, making it even more possible for me to create successes out of ordinary people who otherwise would not have the chance to live their dreams and make it a reality. Anyone with the right mindset, work ethics and proper attitude can make it work for them.

With that said, are you ready for your own success? If the answer is "yes," sit back, relax and enjoy learning about the same 5-step system that has been proven to work for so many before you.

CHAPTER ONE
Why Are You Reading This Book?
*****

Never in a million years would I have imagined that my next book would include a topic as controversial as network marketing. Like many people, I had been brainwashed for a long time about the negative connotations that are associated with the network marketing world.

Before my Internet marketing days, I did dabble in a few network marketing projects. On a few different occasions during my university days, a few friends had actually recommended that I join them in some companies, which I did.

I mean, the opportunities seemed legit, and some of the products were actually pretty good. However, with my natural introverted personality, it did not take long for me to realize that the world of direct sales was simply not for me. I had no interest in meeting and talking to people, and as a result, I failed miserably with every single one of them.

For me personally, it was already difficult enough to socialize with my own family and friends. How would I ever be able to not only talk to complete strangers, but also attempt to sell them something?

Like most people on this planet, I believe this was one of the biggest contributing factors on why I grew up thinking negatively about network marketing. At the time, arranging meetings over coffee or tea, talking to them face-to-face and conducting personal presentations with pamphlets describing the business opportunity were pretty much the only way to sign up any new partners, and that was definitely not my style.

For this reason, as well as my stubborn attitude about avoiding any network marketing or direct sales opportunities proposed to me, I have wasted so many years that could have blossomed so much more spectacularly than it is now.

However, I do believe that everything happens for a reason, and if it was not my time to venture into network marketing at the time, then now is as good a time as any because my years spent in the Internet Marketing community have allowed me to meet so many more business partners and create the success stories needed to make a much bigger impact on the lives of those who come my way.

In addition, my extra years of Internet marketing experience have resulted in a much better online system, which is further enhanced due to my connections made while inside the Internet Marketing circle. That is why I believe everything happens when they are supposed to, and now is the perfect time to take this mission to a whole new level.

Of course, with all the building blocks that have been set up along the way for me to finally produce this book, this brings us back to you. If the series of events had never happened the way they did, I probably would have written this book at another day or time in the past or future, where you may not have been able to grab a copy. See, it all makes sense now.

Ultimately, this then begs us to ask the question: Why are you reading this book? What compelled you to pick up a copy? Can this be the beginning of a big change in your life?

The answer to these questions lies within you. Whether you are aware of it or not, this is the start of something truly amazing. However, in order for that to happen, you must open up your mind to the possibilities and accept the road ahead.

It may not be easy, it may even be challenging, but in the end, you will realize without a shadow of a doubt that it will be worth it.

*****

In order for you to completely understand why you are reading this book, you must first realize what is your ultimate goal for educating yourself. By this, I don't mean what you wish to achieve, because chances are, the first thing that comes to mind is that you want to make more money.

Don't get me wrong, as there is nothing wrong with wanting to make a better living for an improved quality of life for you and your family. Nevertheless, do keep in mind that money is only a means to a way of attaining what you ultimately want.

Consider this. Whether you like to think about it or not, none of us are going to be here in 100 years. Are you going to be able to take the money with you? At that time, will it somehow make a difference whether you made $1.00 or $100,000 a year?

As great as money is, you need to recognize the real reason of everything you are working towards. What is it that will make your life meaningful? Worthwhile? Memorable?

Again, only you would know the answer because your life is your own. It may be that you want to spend more time with your family. It may be that you want to make sure your future generations can be well taken care of with or without you. Or, it may simply be that you want to travel the world and experience some of the best that life has to offer.

At the end, when you are asked how satisfied you are with your life, what memories you have created with your loved ones and the kind of legacy you have left behind, you want to know that whatever course of action you have taken will always be remembered fondly in the minds and hearts of those whom you care about the most in this world.

Friends, this is how you build a dream, a life, a legacy. Once you actually discover your true reason for existence and living your life, then, and only then, will you be ready to put in your very best efforts to turn your best dreams into reality.

*****

It goes without saying that working diligently towards your goals with a never giving up attitude is easier said than done. You know this and I know this. If I were to say this is the one and only true secret to success, I completely understand that I would not be fooling anybody.

Although when you sit back and really reflect on the real reasons of your hard work, you will soon realize that it all makes sense. That is when you will truly comprehend what it is you are fighting so hard to attain, and what you are willing to sacrifice along the way to get there.

When you finally do get there, you will realize that your hard-fought battles all along in the name of providing a better life for yourself and your family are all worth it. The moment you raise your arms in victory and successfully attained the lifestyle freedom that you truly deserve, you know deep down that nothing else can ever stand in your way.

That's because financially, you will be on top of the world. You no longer have to worry about how you will pay for the next bill and whether or not there will be food on the table during your next meal.

On the basis of time, you will be able to spend it however you wish. You can go to sleep and wake up whenever you feel like it, and you will have complete freedom to take the day or week off to spend with your family if you so desired.

It also takes a certain type of personality in order to live this type of freedom where you are 100% in control of your lifestyle. As mentioned before, not everyone is meant to live it, and for those who are not open-minded enough to see the positive aspects of these business models, it is, unfortunately, not for them.

In addition to having an open mind, a successful entrepreneur in this industry must be prepared to learn, willing to invest and be readily coachable. There is no room for ego in this business as every day is a new day for learning, and there will never be any moment when you will officially know everything there is to know about in the world.

When you learn to be passionate and grateful about all that life has already given to you, and you are ready to give back, not only will you be able to make a change in your own life, but also make a huge difference in the world around you.

After you have adjusted your mindset to a more positive way of thinking and looking at opportunities, it is only then that you will you realize you are ready for the next chapter in your life.

CHAPTER CONTRIBUTION #1

The Necessary Attitude To Make USD1000 In One Day From One Hour Of Work Within One Month After Attending First Internet Marketing Course, And Commit So Much To Leadership That Within One Year, Ex-Newbie Now Takes The Stage As A Speaker While Training Team Who Now Calls Him Their Mentor

Contributor: William Cheong
Protégé, Lead Mentor, Team Leader, Speaker, Trainer, Elite Coach

What is the inner game that has driven me to become successful in my Internet Entrepreneur journey? What elements have pushed me to apply my own discipline and to schedule everything in the pipeline while executing them on time?

How did I become successful in only one year in terms of being able to create income online despite starting off as a fresh newbie, then gradually became a leader in my group, their mentor, and even the main trainer for my own class?

Well, this all boils down the one crucial fact: the correct mindset. Many people have a misconception about mindset. Some people might think that getting self-motivated is the correct mindset; some people might think being open-minded to accept every opportunity is the correct mindset.

Does that mean solely being self-motivated and open-minded is enough to achieve this correct mindset? All I can say is: No! Definitely not enough.

Let's first talk about self-motivation. For me personally, self-motivation is the excitement that you can feel, one that you may have felt since the very first day you joined the business.

However, do you have the self-initiative to execute the plan? Can you keep the excitement until the day you become successful? Have you drawn your own Gant chart to complete everything like what you planned on the very first day? Do you have the problem solving skills, or are you just waiting for your mentor or coach to guide you?

The difference between the "entrepreneur" mindset and the "employee" mindset is this:

Entrepreneur-minded individuals always take the initiative to do things on their own. Even when facing challenges, they find their way to solve them. They know how to execute things themselves, find solutions for all the problems, and get the job done themselves instead of waiting for others to spoon feed them.

Employee-minded individuals would wait for others to tell them what to do, pay them some tokens, and make them move. Do you think this is the correct way?

Think of it like somebody who consistently attends Tony Robbins' seminars. Event after event, talk after talk, they are motivated, but motivated to do what? Continue to listen to their boss and follow instructions to do their daily work at a job? Is this called motivation?

Let's take a look at what I have done differently. This is what I have been doing all this time: Whenever I face problems, the first thing I would do is ask Google. If needed, I buy related short courses to adopt the necessary skills that would help me proceed further.

During the beginning stages of my Internet entrepreneurship journey, and being totally new to Facebook Ads, this is exactly what I did: Bought a $25 USD guide that explains which buttons to push on the settings.

Everyone's time is precious, which is why for these small things, I would rather figure out how to solve them myself instead of bugging my mentor or anyone else on these technical parts where the answers can easily be found elsewhere.

Because of this, I have mastered this technical skill on my own. Although regarding the marketing strategy part, you have to ask the right guy instead of Google, as there would be no viable solutions available there that knows my exact situation. In this case, it would be the right time to consult your mentor.

So, the lesson will be: Execute whatever you plan to do, set a deadline and let the countdown timer chase your back, so that you are able to complete your task on time. This is called self-initiative.

Pursue the solution to all the challenges on your own until the stage when you can no longer find a way out. It is only then when it is truly the right time to seek for your mentor's help. This is true self-motivation.

Another part I would like to share is being open-minded. In my observation, many people have mistakenly interpreted Sir Richard Branson's quote: "If somebody offers you an amazing opportunity, but you are not sure you can do it, say yes – then learn how to do it later!"

Well, picking up an opportunity is one thing, but are you open-minded to learning new things? Are you open-minded to getting a coach? Are you open-minded enough to empty your cup and absorb new things from those who have already done it?

A "yes" answer to all of the above is the only way to have a true open-mind. For me, if I decided to pick up an opportunity, I would be open for coaching, willing to listen to all advice, willing to get scolded if I am wrong, willing to throw my entire ego aside and be a humble student. I would be open to learn, to accept, and to improve myself to the next level.

Most of the time, when we first start something, we would go into the wrong path. We would make mistakes, and eventually, need someone to come and guide us.

However, when the person is willing to put aside his time and give you advice, would you execute it? Or would you think twice before doing it? This asks another question: If you don't trust that person, why would you go and find him for advice? After he has given the advice, why would you need to think about it instead of executing it?

Usually, I would use Sir Richard Branson's words in this way: I execute all the suggested actions by my mentor first, then after that, only think and learn why that action is necessary to be taken. With this move, I have saved a lot of time and cut short my path to become an Internet entrepreneur.

In a nutshell, you have to be self-motivated in

terms of having the self-initiative to face challenges, execute plans, and improve yourself. You also must be open-minded in terms of learning, taking advice and execution. Do first, learn later. With these two criteria, your speed to success will be highly accelerated.

CHAPTER CONTRIBUTION #2

Partner Fast Tracks Way To Leadership Success By Upgrading To Protégé Status Within Only Three Months After Signing Up Online, And Is Now An Active Leader, Speaker And Trainer To The Team

Contributor: Andrew Cheah
Protégé, Lead Mentor, Team Leader, Speaker, Trainer, Elite Coach

Within a short three-month period after starting the business by signing up 100% online, I managed to work my way up by becoming the Protégé of my mentor, Simon Leung.

Many fellow team members often ask how they can follow in my footsteps, as they also want the same mentorship and opportunities that fast-tracked my success in this business. Well, the key factor that contributed to this success is mainly by having a certain type of mindset, what I call it the "Champion" mindset.

Most motivation books written by successful

people talks about mindset. If you do not believe me, find a business or success book inside any bookstore right now and flip to the table of contents, and you can see that a big portion of the book usually talks about having the right mindset.

However, to a lot of people who wants to learn from these motivation books, techniques and tools are more important. Plus, they feel that the mindset thing is not important because most of these authors share almost the same mindset content.

Let me ask you a question. If there is a class of students who have the same knowledge and skills, why is it that only a few of them become successful while others don't? The reason is mainly due to the mindset that they have.

I know the importance of having the Champion mindset because I am a corporate coach. The key to getting anyone to become successful is to challenge them to have the proper way of thinking like a true winner.

When I first started this business, I already knew that I had to be successful so that I can help others, and one way to be successful is to be a leader. My secret to success is very simple and I learned it from the Bible.

"Give, and it will be given to you" – Luke 6:38

If you want to learn, prepare to teach, because

when you learn as if you are going to teach others, then you will absorb better.

If you want to be a leader, then you must start serving others because when you serve others, you gain their respect and you automatically grow to be a leader. If you want someone to be your mentor, you must ask yourself what you can do for him or her.

As a total newbie to this industry in the beginning, I made sure to do a lot of research and read many books on how to become successful in this business. It's not only to succeed myself, but so that I can teach others to be successful, too.

Once I have this knowledge, I quickly practiced what I learned. You know what? It worked. Then, I started to become a trainer and whenever possible, I would train or share with the team on the techniques that worked.

I continued to learn and teach others, and my best satisfaction comes from my partners who have practiced what I taught them, who all told me how happy they were when they finally saw their business grow as a result of my teachings.

The world is an interesting place. The "Law of Giving" shapes my life and business, too. When you start doing that without expecting anything in returns, you will receive in abundance.

The Law of Giving plays a more significant role in this business because this is the business of helping others to become better in terms of health, beauty and wealth. When I started to help my mentor and others, then I started to learn more and grow.

Once you have this Champion mindset, the next thing you need to have is persistence. A business is like growing a tree. It takes time to grow, so we need to continue to water, nurture and provide nutrients until you can see the shoots grow from the soil and slowly become a tree.

Like anything in life, such as growing a tree or building a business, do not give up too fast when you still have not seen the results. In fact, this is an indication that you need to be more persistent to work harder.

Now you know the kind of mindset that drives me to become the best that I can be, it is now my challenge to you to start developing your own Champion mindset to become successful. Anyone can also fast track their way to success. Just make sure you are mentally prepared for the challenge ahead.

CHAPTER CONTRIBUTION #3

Stay-At-Home Mom Shares The Importance Of Understanding That This Is Ultimately A Products Business, And How To Effectively Mold The Mindset Of All Partners That They Need To Use, Consume And Invest In The Products In Order To Expand Their Business

Contributor: Ming Liang
Protégé, Lead Mentor, Team Leader, Speaker, Trainer, Elite Coach

Regardless of the business, I strongly feel that we have to learn to see it from the perspective of the customers. We need to understand their perceptions and how they feel or think, then establish the right marketing strategies from the customer's point of view.

For a successful business, this is an important piece of the puzzle. For example, there may be a website designer who comes to tell you how important it is to have a website for a business in this new era, and what benefits your business will get as a result.

However, when you look at his name card, there's no website URL stated on the card. Furthermore, when you ask him for his website address, he replies, "Oh, we don't have it yet." What's on your mind when this happens?

Firstly, you would definitely feel that this person is not professional enough to share with you why a website is important to your business because he himself also doesn't even have one for his own business.

Another thing in your mind might be "Are you sure that he can even deliver a completed website?"

In the network marketing business, there are at least 4 reasons why we should be consuming our own products.

Reason Number One: Because I am the boss in this business!

Whenever you are running a business, other people may ask you what business you are doing. If your answer is anti-aging, then their eyes immediately will focus on your face and skin.

If your answer is health, then their mind will immediately wonder how healthy you are. If your answer is slimming, their eyes will immediately scan you thoroughly from head to toe to check out how fit you are, while guessing what your figure is or what size you are wearing.

This is normal human reaction, and we can't blame them. We can only do our best. That's why for every single one of my new partners who come in to our business, I will advise them to use the products, and to always be a consumer first.

Not only that, but also to take pictures before they use the products, and compare this with the after. This is to show the people who are curious on their improvements along the way.

Simply put, we are not only the bosses of our business. Rather, we are also the ambassadors of our own products. Let me give you an example.

You have two boss friends. Let's call them Boss A and Boss B. Both are selling V-face masks.

They know you are looking for something that can help make faces look contour and V-shape, so they come to talk to you.

Boss A has many products in his company, but he never tried out any of them. When he talks to you, he is trying to read the instructions on the packaging.

Boss B, on the other hand, has only one series of products in his company. The difference is that he is using his company's products everyday and he loves his products very much.

He is also teaching you his ways regarding how to use the products effectively. He shares with you his own experience after using the products and also his reasons for starting this business in the first place.

After a close comparison, both products turn out to be about the same in terms of quality and cost, with no special offers from either side. The only differences are the bosses and your experience with them.

Who would you buy from?

If you are like most people, you would choose Boss B. Why? When you figure out the answer, you would understand exactly why you should start using the products you are selling.

Reason Number Two: Speak confidently.

If we want our businesses to go long and far, we must do this business honestly. We cannot lie to our customers if we do not use the products, simply because customers would know it if you are dishonest with them.

Let's say you successfully lied to them today, but in the days that follow, they may continue to ask you many more questions about your products. These may be questions that you are not familiar with, so you have difficulties understanding their situations and providing them with the right answers.

If you can't guide them to use the products effectively or show them the results they expected, then very soon, they are not going to consume or use your products anymore. To say it bluntly, in the perspective of your customers, your products are scams!

This is a very serious mistake if you actually did this. Should you be lucky enough to encounter a Mr. or Ms. Nice who happens to be able to tolerate your empty promises and not pursue the matter, then perhaps you are safe.

On the other hand, if you are not so lucky, he or she is going to tell everybody that your products are a huge scam, and that you are an even bigger scammer. Plus, with social media advancement nowadays, your entire business will be affected.

Now, let's look at this in another way. If you are using the products and love the products, your business will fly. That's because you understand well about the products you are selling, and you know the exact healing process, how to use them, and how to apply them effectively.

Hence, whenever people ask you any related questions about the products, you easily understand them and are able to answer their questions well.

From my experience, I use our own products daily with all my family members, and I have also personally tried each and every one of the products, even the ones that are not currently available in my own country.

The end result is that I have gained back my health and youthful looks. For my baby, the products have also gotten rid of her nose and skin sensitivity. I use the products on her all the time whenever she has problems, and they quickly resolve them.

I share my experiences with my business partners, who also share their experiences back to me. You know what? They, too, have also informed me their improvements, not only from themselves, but from their loved ones and babies, as well.

Ever since growing our businesses to many cities and countries, I have been receiving countless thank you's, show of appreciation, and even more testimonials regarding how my customers and partners gained back their health.

And now, at each and every one of my product presentations or sharing sessions, I can also answer any question that our prospects may ask about the products with ease, and without any hesitation at all.

My customers are not only buying, but they are also sharing with their friends and family about the products that I introduced to them, all confidently and happily without stress.

As an Internet marketer, I also believe that using products is a very important process when you are looking for the right marketing ideas. Without using the products, you may encounter difficulties when trying to write a good salesletter or establishing a suitable marketing strategy to help you sell more products.

Reason Number Three: We all dream of closing sales without opening our mouths.

I have a partner who gives away the products to her mother. The mother has been using our products for a few months. One day, two relatives come to their house for a visit, and they happened to notice her mother's face has changed.

Yes, changed. It changed to looking younger. Her pores became smaller, and she even has fewer wrinkles.

Shocked, her relatives asked, "What are you using? I also want to use!" After the mother showed the relatives her skin care products, the relatives immediately ordered 2 sets from her.

The most interesting and ironic part of this story is that the mother actually has zero knowledge about the products, and she has absolutely no sales experience at all. Yes, having product knowledge is good, but evidently, it is not necessary, as proven in this situation.

In addition, we also have a few partners who were critical illness patients in the past, and they also shared very similar experiences. Visitors who had seen them while they were thought to be in their final moments were stunned when the patients actually began to show signs of improving health. In the end, the visitors also turned into their new customers.

Reason Number Four: Replicable business.

The world can be a huge place if you want your business to be covered worldwide. To do this, you definitely cannot try to be a hero or heroine. Instead, you must be a good team player and a good leader.

Build a team and fight together, because the power of 10 is so much bigger and stronger than the power of 1. In order for your team to grow, you must let them be "another you."

This means you need to let them be a duplicate of you and turn into another leader. In the progress of duplication, they will inevitably copy many of the things that you will be doing.

So, if you want them to speak about the products confidently like you, then you should allow them to replicate how you use the products and how you love the products.

With that said, if you don't use the products daily, they would also follow your actions exactly. If you feel that using products is not important in this business, then everyone under you would also feel the same way.

On the other hand, if you commit to using the products daily and extending the usage to your friends and family, then your partners would also use the products daily and extend the usage to their friends and family, too.

Remember, the more they consume, the more your business will be growing, and the more testimonials you will be collecting. All the testimonials you have collected are your teasers. Different teasers are used to catch different fishes.

Of course, you have to share and clone the methods on how you catch the fishes with your fellow leaders, too. The more skills you duplicate to them, the more fishes they would have.

At this point, can you visualize the impact of using products yet? Imagine for one moment how much you would have lost if you are not using the products, and how much more you would have gained if you did.

Be responsible and do the right thing. Commit to your own business. Use your own products, and watch your business bloom.

CHAPTER TWO
How To Collect Unlimited Names And Contact Details Online Like Virtual Business Cards

*****

You can choose to do it the easy way, or you can choose to do it the hard way. Unfortunately, if you want to do it the right way, you will not be able to find a shortcut, at least not in the initial set up of your online system.

The good news is that in this section, we will be discussing the system so you can understand how it works technologically. The bad news is whether you like it or not, you will eventually need to set one up, so it is pointless to prolong the inevitable.

Although upon the completion of your online system setup, the best news of all is that you will no longer need to worry about it. From that point forward, everything will be as smooth as butter, and assuming you have a talented team to help you out, everything you need to do will be a piece of cake.

In actuality, if you are not adamant about automating your online lead generation process, developing a way for you to collect leads online actually is not all that difficult.

Even though automation is not a requirement to build your business online, in a later chapter, we will still discuss the benefits of running as much of your business as possible on autopilot, as well as how you can do it should you have an interest.

Before we begin, I'm sure you can think of several ways for you to collect names and contact details with very little technical set up. For example, you simply request that they get sent to you via email, social media, private messages, chats or whatever other platform that you use.

On the other hand, if you recall that one of our goals is to share with you how to network and even potentially sign up new customers or partners without personal communication, we will need to put together an online system capable of doing that.

Now, don't have a panic attack just yet. I'm not asking you to develop the technology required to make this work, as the tools already exist. All I am doing is directing you to the right platforms and share with you a few ways I have done this.

Ready? Let's get this over with!

*****

For Internet newbies with zero technical knowledge, the most practical online tool you can use are website creators that require no programming on your end. In fact, the majority of the tools comprise mostly of dragging and dropping website elements you want on your page.

After several minor customizations, which may include your text, personal images and color preferences, the entire thing is uploaded onto an existing website server. With your own personal URL, anyone can now visit that link and view the webpage that you have created in about 20 minutes.

The best part about most of these website creator tools is that the use of their service, and even hosting your webpage directly on their servers, are completely free of charge.

This means you are able to create as many webpages as you want, or include different variations of a webpage that may be promoting different things.

Because this service costs you nothing, how you plan to use it is entirely up to you, assuming that your content comply with the service's terms and conditions.

While there are literally hundreds or even thousands of free website creators to choose from, you may want to consider some that belong to the top names in the tech world. This is because these companies will take more serious measures in terms of improving their service quality, providing better tools, as well as protecting the security of the sites.

To give you an idea on some of the ones I personally use, they include Google Sites, Blogger, Wordpress, and Instapage, just to name a few. If you want to find more, a simple Google search on "free website builder," "free website creator" or "create free websites" will deliver you more results than you will have time to try.

Because there are already countless tutorials on how to use these websites that are readily available online, along with hundreds of step-by-step videos you can find on YouTube, I will not explain how to use these tools here.

Rather, I would like to point out all these tools have the capability for the website creator to use a built-in drag and drop element or plugin to collect names and contact details directly on your website. Then, when somebody does enter in your requested details on your form, the information will be emailed to you.

A good rule of thumb to keep in mind is that in the real world, most people would not willingly submit their names and contact information to just anybody on the world wide web for no reason. I'm sure you value your privacy as much as everyone else, so you can understand that only having a form requesting for people's contact details on your website simply would not work.

The way that you will convince somebody to hand over their private information to you is by giving them something valuable in exchange. As far as what you can ethically bribe them with, this will be explained later in chapter four.

In the meantime, simply understand that the technology required to make this work is readily available for free in some of the most popular website creation tools in the world. All you need to do is explore a bit to figure out how to set it all up.

Once you spend a little time playing around with the website creation tools, you will realize that it is actually quite easy to build your website. Who knows, maybe you will even have some fun doing it in the process.

Note: Should you require additional assistance in

this process or any of the other ones explained in later chapters, feel free to check out the "Resources" section towards the end of this book.

*****

Another way to collect leads without any technical set up is to simply use social networking, such as Facebook. While there is currently no simplified way for just anybody to create a form that asks users to enter in their personal details, you are still able to contact them any time you wish simply by having them connect with you via social networks.

We will talk more about various Facebook marketing techniques in chapter five, but in the meanwhile, simply understand that social networking is another very powerful tool for you to not only communicate, but keep in touch and ultimately contact anyone in your prospect list.

There are several ways in which you can connect with people on Facebook. The most obvious way is to first send them friend requests and become friends with them. Once you are officially connected, this will allow you to see their posts and images on your newsfeed, and vice versa.

As friends, you can easily interact with them by

liking, commenting and even sharing their posts. You are able to initiate conversations with them by commenting on their posts, leaving feedback or asking open-ended questions about their content.

In addition, for those with whom you have already made a connection, you can be sure that any private messages you send them will be delivered to their inbox. Even though you have the capability to send personal messages to anyone who activates this function, it is possible that your message will get filtered if you are not friends with that person.

For this reason, it cannot be guaranteed that your message will go through if you do not first send that person a friend request. A good rule of thumb is that if you want to contact somebody personally, always make the initial connection first as a friend, then only proceed with your private chats.

Unfortunately, there may be times when sending a friend request may not be possible. For example, the person has already reached his or her friend limit (Facebook only allows 5000 friends per account), the individual has not yet responded to your request (or declined it), or maybe the "friend request" option has been deactivated by the user.

In most cases, you are still able to "follow" the user, which means that while you are not officially friends on Facebook, you will still be able to see this person's public posts in your newsfeed. This is convenient if you know you want to interact with this person from time to time, and would like to leave comments on his or her future posts.

Yet another way to build a following is to use Facebook's wide variety of other platforms. This includes creating a Facebook Page where you can attract an unlimited amount of "likes" from fans, or by creating Facebook Groups on a variety of topics that will draw the membership of anyone with similar interests, hobbies or businesses.

When other Facebook users are connected to your Page or members of your Group, you are also able to communicate with them directly by making new posts inside the Pages and Groups. This is a great way for mass communicating when friending somebody is not an option.

Because of your ability to communicate with countless users, Facebook is one of the best ways for you to keep track of all your leads, prospects and potential future partners. When the time is right and you have something to show them, simply make another new post or send a private message to them, and then await their responses.

There is virtually no limit to how many people you

can connect with on Facebook, which means you can collect as many of them as you want.

*****

Later on in this book, we will further discuss how to drive traffic to your lead generation website. In the meanwhile, you can continue to explore how to collect your leads.

Even though Facebook is one of the most popular platforms for you to connect with potential prospects, it does not necessarily promise that those who come across your Page or profile would take the first step to connect with you. As a matter of fact, hundreds or even thousands may find you, but out of every one person who adds or likes you, another ten or more may have simply clicked away, never to be seen or heard from again.

In Internet marketing, the most important thing that you can do is to have a system capable of collecting the contact details from your leads. This must be in a much more proactive manner that specifically requesting this information from your visitors.

On Facebook, there is no built-in way to do this. Even when different features are used to activate this functionality, the form is typically in the middle of a lot of other distractions that will affect the focus of your visitor and impact your conversion, including other posts, links and ads that are all around that form.

For this reason, having another webpage dedicated to the collecting of leads would work infinitely better. However, not everyone wants to or knows how to create his or her own lead generation webpage. This is where some additional third-party tools will come in handy.

Earlier, we had touched on various tools that allow you to create any type of website that you want for free. Along the same lines, if your intention is to generate leads by collecting people's names, email address, phone number, address or pretty much any other piece of information you want, I have another good recommendation for you.

Whenever I want to generate leads with a ready-made system that is already designed to collect personal information, I use a tool called Eventbrite. Eventbrite is quite popular among many event organizers as well as attendees, and it is widely used to promote online or offline events.

Regardless of what it is that you are promoting, the main benefit of this tool is that the lead generation process is already built right into the system. You are even able to use it to create your own webpage online, and any visitor around the world would be able to access the website.

There are countless features with this platform, particularly the flexibility you have to create and design your own promotional page on the Internet. After people register for your event, their contact details are automatically sent to you, and you also have the option to have emails sent to them on autopilot.

Of course, this should be used only if you actually do have an event to promote, as this platform is designed as a promotional tool for event organizers, as well as attendees in search of seminars.

Later on, we will discuss more on what events you can promote and how to best attract the right market for your business. In addition, we will also talk about the importance of using emails as a way to communicate and follow up with your registrants.

CHAPTER CONTRIBUTION #1

Basic Lead Generation Training Allows Partner To Use Existing Technology To Grow A Facebook Page From 100+ Fans To 2000+ Fans Within Just Months

Contributor: Andrew Cheah
Protégé, Lead Mentor, Team Leader, Speaker, Trainer, Elite Coach

When I started this online business, I followed the training developed by the gurus because they have already done that, which means I don't have to go through the trial and error phase. To me, it is a no-brainer to follow the steps taught in the trainings.

Tony Robbins always says that "success leaves traces," and I strongly agree with him. I just followed the steps in the training, and while watching the videos, I simply paused them to follow exactly the processes taught.

One of the lessons I learned is to build leads through Facebook Pages. I had an old Facebook Page that I created some time ago, and it took me more than one year to get around to more than 100 fans before this training.

I then followed the steps from the training and applied the strategies to the same old fan page. Suddenly, my fans started to grow slowly at the initial stage and after a week or two, more and more fans liked my page.

Within only months, my fans have grown from around 100+ to more than 3000 now. The simple training really amazed me in its effectiveness.

Another even more exciting news happened soon afterwards. One day, I received an email notification, which informed me that I have made a sale of USD250. Wow!

I know this is not a huge amount, but I can assure you that this moment was one of my happiest moments because it showed me that my efforts were worth it, and the training really works.

The interesting part is that I am only half way though the training program and with all my time traveling for my other businesses and watching the training only in my spare time, all of this, including my results, all happened in less than 90 days within starting this business.

We must be aware that if a training is created by experienced experts, everything is created based on their experience. At least, this is the way I created my own trainings. I would always provide tips on what to do and what not to do because I have tried those methods or have gone through the processes already.

Therefore, I only choose to work with experienced mentors because they have the knowledge and experience that will help me to become better.

Once I decide to work with them, I will trust them and their trainings. I won't question their materials and will follow through until I can learn, execute and get the results.

Remember that if you would like to get real results, you need to put in real action. Do not just learn without execution. Learning alone will not get you results. Only execution will.

Personally, I always follow the process of "Learn - Do - Improve," which was taught by my mentor at a live team training where I was also one of his co-trainers for two days. Learning and executing must come hand-in-hand so that you can get the results.

If the result is good, then you know that you are on the right track. However, if the result is not what you expected, then you have to improve on your steps or actions.

This is a simple method that can and will bring you closer to success, but a lot of people think the concept is too simple, so they end up not believing it would work.

Henry Ford said, "Whether you think you can, or you think you can't, you're right." Well, if anyone thinks that the concept would not work for them, then they are right. It would not work for them, not because it does not work, but because they don't believe that it works.

Now, the time is right, and we have the tools and even training steps that are simple enough for most people to follow. Most importantly, they are effective.

With the training and system, I am now enjoying US Dollar passive income and I can say that I now have my dream business. To me, this is just the beginning because when I started this business less than 6 months ago (at the time of this writing), I could already see the great potential in this business.

I strongly know that this business will help me to achieve the freedom that I want, which is to travel and work whenever and wherever I desire. More so, I really hope to help others, especially my friends who are still working or "surviving" in the corporate world, to enjoy the freedom I now enjoy.

CHAPTER CONTRIBUTION #2
■■■

How To Create An Effective Facebook Lead Generation Profile Or Page By Embedding Content, Building Bridge Pages And Using Other Available Features

Contributor: Mine Vinc
Team Leader, Speaker, Elite Member

If you are a business owner or entrepreneur, you probably know that you need to be on social networks such as Facebook. This is all I use to build my home business, and I now have partners all around the world even though I am in Singapore.

This platform is considered one of the most active in terms of interaction for connecting people together, including friends or followers, family, people who share similar interests, and even your business partners.

It is also a place where you can brand yourself and can be used as a communication medium to connect with your customers on business functions.

Facebook is just like a website with an open

network and is built on the basis that everyone within your social circle can see everything that everyone else is doing.

Over the past few years, this platform has become the favorite tool for Internet marketers or online entrepreneurs to craft and build their business strategies.

A Facebook profile is mainly for individuals and is for non-commercial use. It represents an individual person and must be held under an individual name that can be interacted with friends and followers.

The first thing that people always do is to check your profile before they associate it with you. Therefore, it is important that you create the right kind of profile.

Your photo on your profile should be a real photo of you because people want to interact with real people. This is Facebook, after all, and if they see that your profile is using a logo, pet or pretty scenery, likely they won't want to be friends with you.

Therefore, it is important that you make sure your profile is inviting and attractive. Facebook allows you to have a maximum of 5000 friends and an unlimited number of followers.

Since you can only add 5000 friends on Facebook, your profile should also tell a story, so be yourself and share some hobbies or things that you like to do.

In the "About Me" section, you can write 2 or 3 paragraphs on how you got to where you are. With limited space in the profile, you can also use it to show off your personality, as well as personal details like your profession, website, and hometown.

Facebook Pages look similar to a Facebook profile, but are created and managed by users within their own profiles. Facebook Pages are not separate Facebook accounts, but rather, an option to create Facebook Pages is available for any Facebook profile.

This function offers unique tools for connecting people to the topics that they care about, such as a business, brand to showcase your work, organization and most importantly, to interact with your fans. The major benefit is you can have unlimited of fans.

Facebook is a useful tool for sharing news and information about your business products, services or events with your friends and public. One of the many ways you can do this is copy and paste the website address (URL). This is also the easiest way to share something, and Facebook will automatically create a preview of the content you're sharing.

Make sure to include the "http://" part of the address. If you are pasting the URL of your landing page into a new post on your Timeline, a preview will appear after a moment. The preview helps to get clicks as it will give your friends an idea on what the website is about before they click on it.

Once you have pasted the URL of your landing page into a new post on your or someone else's Timeline, you can delete the URL after the preview is generated. Even after you delete it, the preview will still be there, allowing anyone to click on it, except they won't see the ugly URL in your post.

By the way, it is good to note that if you are pasting a URL into a comment or a chat, no preview will appear at first, but one will be created when you post it.

If you want to embed an existing post, even a video post, you just click in the top right corner. There, you will see an option to embed post. Once you've clicked on the option to embed post, a code will come up.

All you need to do is copy that code, and then paste it into your post. This doesn't work for every post on Facebook unless you set your privacy to public, so make sure the world icon is there before you go trying to embed an update.

Most Facebook users are very active, many posting their activities while they interact with friends, join in on discussions, browse through photo galleries, check out what's going on in their groups and often clicking on URL links.

With the billions of users who are actively participating on this social site, most of them use the platform multiple times every single day. The traffic is already there, and most of the online entrepreneurs make use of these advantages to tag into Facebook as a platform to build their businesses.

Virtually every businessperson today has a Facebook page and you can be sure to generate more leads to your business purposes.

In order for you to do that, it is essential for you to create a Facebook Page to connect with their potential prospects and generate more leads to the business. Your Page allows you to share your knowledge in your niche and build relationship with people.

Facebook definitely has the potential to generate leads when used correctly. When you simply share and never try to push your products on them, they may be interested in partnering with you in your business.

With that said, you need to share your value, story, activities and your ability to help others. This is what will really drive the process of finding people once they know about your business.

After you know what the value is, one of the methods that I use to generate leads is set-up a landing page on your Facebook. In order for you run your

Facebook Ads effectively, you need to have a bridge page where you can place your landing page on your Facebook page tabs.

First, what is bridge page?

Bridge pages basically allow you to promote your offer by using Facebook Ads and have higher possibility of being approved by Facebook. With this feature, you can have 3 options, including static page, video page and landing page (Opt-in page).

You can also use bridge pages to promote your sales funnel. If you had set up the landing page properly on your Facebook, chances are people will tend to see your offer either on the tab or at the side of your favorites section.

If you are using Facebook Ads, the leads will be directed to the bridge page where they can see all the promotions that you are offering. You should promote only one thing on each bridge page for best results.

In conclusion, if you are serious in building your business, I strongly encourage you to set up your Facebook profile correctly and make this a better platform to connect with more people who need help.

CHAPTER CONTRIBUTION #3

An Accountant Preparing For Retirement Finds A New Source Of Internet Income Through Driving International Leads With Only Facebook To A Free Lead Generation Platform

Contributor: Elaine Pang
Team Speaker, Elite Member

As a business owner since 1997, I needed to find a new source of income outside of a time-demanding accounting service in preparation for retirement. I wanted something more passive and exponential in nature, and I cannot see myself sitting at home not doing anything except watching TV all the time.

One day, while I was browsing Facebook, I saw a post that caught my interest. It was actually a Facebook ad that appeared on my newsfeed. The post read something like this:

"[LAST EVENT OF 2015 IN KL] Discover Insider Secrets To Making USD Online. Internet Marketing's "Insider" From USA Returns To KL For

The LAST Time This Year!"

I was curious about the topic, so I clicked on the button that says "Learn More," which brought me to the page to register for a seminar promoting my mentor, Simon Leung. The webpage was created using Eventbrite.

As I read the content of the website, the professional copywriting really captivated me, so much so that I felt it was talking directly to me. I was quickly attracted by the content of the seminar, and thus registered for it.

I attended the 3-hour seminar presented by my future mentor and immediately signed up for business opportunity offered on that day. Since I started this online business, I have started to earn in USD dollars, mainly from customers who saw my ad on their Facebook newsfeed.

When Facebook users see my ad, they click on it only to be redirected to an Eventbrite page created and professionally written by my mentor. It didn't take me long to realize that this was the exact same process that I went through, which means that this is a proven system as it had worked on me.

Eager to replicate the process, but this time for myself, I began to explore into the powerful marketing strategy called Facebook Ads because I myself got attracted to the business by first responding to an ad. So I got my mentor to teach me how to craft a compelling ad that can attract people to click on it, and thus land on the event registration page that had been created for our team.

In a short period of time, I actually managed to send people to attend our business previews in Singapore, Jakarta, Penang and KL. All of them were sent to the same registration page as soon as they clicked on the ad.

Without Facebook Ads, I would not have been able to reach the International market. And without Eventbrite, I would not have had such a powerful platform to promote, which, combined with the skillful copywriting by my mentor, helped me to easily earn USD income online.

To my surprise, I ended up being labeled a "rare species" among my team members for being able to attract a high number of people to attend the event just through one ad. Thanks to the registration system, they were able to register for the seminar, and then signing them up for the business opportunity on the spot.

Facebook Ads and Eventbrite are effective approaches to get a lead to take action. You can specify the desired potential customers – their age group, location, interests, occupation and gender. Then,

Facebook will only deliver the ad to the newsfeed of those people who met the criteria set by you so you know that your registration page is related to what they want.

As an advertiser, you only pay for the cost of the ads (as determined by Facebook) when an action has taken place, either when the Facebook user clicks on the ads, or when the Facebook ads have been shown an X number of times. You can set a budget at which the ad will be stopped from being shown. From an accountant's viewpoint, this is a quantifiable cost.

In the beginning, I didn't do proper targeting and got thousands of people clicking on my ad, but they were not interested in the event that I was promoting. Under the guidance of my mentor, I then tweaked the ad by narrowing the target group to ensure that the content of the registration page would speak to them, just like how it spoke to me.

Another thing that will affect the performance of the ad is the image you use for your ad. Once, I had this ad with an image that I thought would attract people to click on it. Instead, nobody clicked on the ad, not until my mentor advised me to change the image to something that was relevant to the content of the registration page.

With Facebook ads, you are able to test and

measure your promotional campaign. You can create multiple ads, with different wordings and images, and test which ads generate the most number of leads, as well as highest number of registrations for the event.

Before I learned about using Facebook to do marketing, I was using Facebook primarily as a social platform. I was sharing photos of food and places I visited. Now, I still do that, but I also learned to post 'teaser' contents as well, all of which are ultimately designed to direct users to the registration system.

Facebook and Eventbrite have indeed given me an opportunity to get leads from any location I want while sending them to the page I want them to see. My business will continue to grow exponentially, as more and more people log in to use both of these giant social platform tools.

CHAPTER THREE
This Is What You Will Be Doing Online All Day Long
*****

As a network marketer who builds the business online, what exactly will be done on a day-to-day basis? The answer is simple: lead generation.

That's right. Every single day, your only task is to get as many eyeballs onto your webpage as humanly possible. The more visitors you can attract, the more leads you will possibly generate who will hear about your products. This ultimately means more new partners you will potentially sign up.

Now, in order for you to attract people to your website, you will need to learn how to "drive traffic," as we call it in the Internet marketing world. This essentially means that you need to somehow spread the word about your webpage to as many people as you possibly can, hoping that they will see your page and take action on there.

Traffic generation is a skill all by itself, and there are courses on pretty much any kind of traffic generation strategy available. This ranges from free methods to paid methods, as well as using various platforms to attract visitors from.

Unfortunately, we do not currently have the time to go through every traffic source known to man, as the information is too much and will steer us off-topic. However, to give you a general idea, popular strategies include search engine optimization, pay-per-click advertising, classified ads, article marketing, blogging, press releases, e-zine marketing, social media marketing, video marketing and forum marketing, among countless others.

Most, if not all, of these traffic generation strategies will require their own lengthy courses just to get you introduced and accustomed to them, much less properly trained to achieve reasonable results. Not to mention, many of the strategies include the implementation of techniques such as professional writing, creating videos or other technical tasks that may take a while before you can see any results.

Because of the amount of time required for you

to learn these techniques and see results, I will instead be sharing with you the top traffic generation strategies that anybody can do with minimal training and even no experience.

For your information, these are the strategies that I also use almost every single day, and it is also the same information we teach my team, which has resulted in huge success and new signups from all of them who have implemented the techniques, so definitely do not take them lightly, and put it into action the moment you have set up your system.

What is this elite online method that I speak of? Here's the good news. It's most likely something you use every single day and will not need any training on how to use it: Facebook.

With over 1.5 billion users, Facebook is undoubtedly one of the biggest goldmines you can tap into when it comes to online lead generation. Whether you are directly connected with them or not, certain Facebook marketing strategies still allow your promotional messages to reach the newsfeeds of whomever you choose to target.

While there are free Facebook marketing methods available for anyone to use, the paid advertising strategies are also worth exploring because the use of advertisements allows your promotions to reach anyone, anywhere around the world, regardless of whether or not you are friends with them.

*****

First, let us take a deeper look at the free method. The free way to promote on Facebook is nothing more than making the right posts strategically over time, designed to peak the interest of your existing friends or followers.

As a side note, it is good to observe that you need to have a reasonable amount of friends in order for this strategy to work. After all, if we are making promotional posts intended to attract our friends, what good will it do if there are no friends on our list to attract in the first place?

With this in mind, you should aim to continue to add new friends into your Facebook account all the time. I recommend sending out about 5 to 10 new friend requests throughout the course of a day, ideally to those who have mutual friends as you. This way, it does not look like you are simply adding random people with no connection to you.

When you add friends, be careful not to go overboard with too many requests, as it can get your account flagged by Facebook. Sometimes, certain sensitive people may also complain that they received a friend request from somebody they do not know, so you may want to increase your chances of acceptance by sending them messages, liking or commenting on any of their public posts.

The other way to do this is to create your own Facebook Page or Group, which is properly branded as you and focusing on all your business efforts. Similarly, you will need to make sure you have enough followers who "like" your Page and members added into your Group in order for this to work.

While keeping your activities normal and posting as you would usually be posting, sneak in different types of "teaser" content from time to time. Examples could be a photo with your mentor, training sessions you have attended with your team members, or expressing your excitement for some cool things that are up and coming.

When done correctly, your friends will undoubtedly notice, and while they may or may not comment on your post at that moment in time, it is already engraved in their mind that you are doing something that may be of interest to them in the future. This will increase the chances of them contacting you later on to learn more.

At some point, when you actually have

something to invite them to, they will be more prone to express interest because they have already been exposed to your teaser posts previously. Some of them may even be secretly waiting for an event invitation from you, but have been shy to ask.

Once you reach the point where you have an event to invite your prospects to, you can create a Facebook Events page where you can provide the details of the live event and invite all your friends to attend and meet with you in person.

If you make this Event public, it becomes viewable by anyone who happens to be in that area, share the same interests as the topics you have indicated, or have searched on Facebook using similar words as those used in your listing. This is yet another way to generate more attention to your postings.

For ideas on what you can post for your promotional messages or what types of events you can create, stay tuned for the next chapter.

*****

In addition to posting on your own timeline, pages or groups, you also have the capability to post on the ones that belong to your friends. However, just because you have the capability to do it, it is strongly advisable that you do not do this unless you have received permission from your friends first.

One of the worst forms of Facebook etiquette is invading your friends' timelines by posting uninvited content on their walls, or tagging them in posts, photos and videos that they are not in. Some may even "hijack" existing posts by blatantly promoting products and services in the comments.

This is the typical behavior of most people who SPAM, and you do not want to be lumped into this category. Especially with people you do not know or may not be close with, they will easily complain about your antics and put your account in jeopardy.

Similarly, when first starting out and looking for groups to join or pages to like, do so sparingly and just like sending out new friend requests, be careful not to over do it. Facebook will flag your account if you are requesting to join too many groups in a short amount of time, and will eventually prevent you from requesting to join groups and liking new pages, so definitely be weary of that.

However, once approved to join these groups, assuming that it is compliant with the rules set up by the group and page admins, you are free to post anything relevant you wish, under the condition that it is acceptable inside that group.

Some groups may require your posts to be reviewed and approved prior to going live, while other groups may prevent regular members from posting all together. Whatever the case, these are situations we cannot control, so your best bet is to either await approval or move on to another group.

The content that you post should be similar to what you would be posting on your own timeline, page or groups. The only difference is that now, you are posting inside groups with more members, thus increasing the exposure of your ad to a much larger audience on Facebook.

Again, when you are ready for actual promotions as opposed to only posting teaser content all the time, the next chapter will get you ready on what you can post.

*****

Finally, no section on Facebook is complete without the mention of Facebook Ads, which is an advertising platform you can use to expand your reach to people you do not even know on this popular social network.

You have the option to write new ads from scratch and upload your own images, or you can choose to promote your own Facebook page, boost certain posts from those pages, or even give your event pages more exposure by running ads on them.

With the flexibility on Facebook Ads, you can select your market based on their locations, interests, demographics, age, gender and more, which gives you full control of the exact kind of person you would like to target.

On a strategic standpoint, it is recommended for you to target the appropriate geographical locations of your offers. For example, if you are looking for local partners whom you can easily meet up with and have regular discussions, you should not target areas that are not close to you.

Understanding your products is also important for choosing the right target market. For example, if you are selling beauty products, you may not want to target young men who probably have no interest in skincare products.

When writing your ads, you should also keep in mind what you are promoting, and make sure that your ad's marketing message is relevant to what is being offered on the page that visitors will land on once they click on your ad.

For example, if you are sending users to your products, make sure you talk about the products in your ad. Similarly, if you are sending users to a page where they will need to register for an event, make sure you hype up the importance of that event and encourage them to register so they do not miss out on a supposed once-in-a-lifetime event extravaganza.

As far as budget is concerned, this is also within your control, as you can set it to as high or as low as you want. Now, it goes without saying that the higher your budget, the farther your potential reach to make your ads visible to a larger audience, so just keep that in mind in case you are thinking to set your budget to only a few dollars a day, only to realize that your ad's exposure did not reach its full potential.

If you are familiar with your numbers and understand how much profit you will make from every converted customer or new partner signup, then it is in your best interest to set a higher budget so you can generate more leads.

At which time, focus on converting the leads into sales, and you will be ready to generate leads all day long with the objective of turning them into new business partners.

*****

Ultimately, the main idea here is to use

Facebook to generate as many leads as you can. However, in order for you to generate leads, you must have something that you can offer them.

In business, there is no marketing term that is more powerful than the word "free." As you read on to the next chapter, you will discover how you can use the power of free to your advantage in your network marketing business.

CHAPTER CONTRIBUTION #1
■■■

Traditional Network Marketer Applies New Methods With Facebook Ads, Posts, Groups, Pages, And Personal Invitations Via Online Platforms With Great Success

Contributor: Joshua Koay
Team Leader, Speaker, Elite Member

If you are one of the traditional network marketers out there, you know and understand that one of the challenges you will usually face is generating leads.

Well, when it comes to this point, I know some people out there might thought that getting sales or signing up is much more important. While I agree that both of them are indeed important, have you ever thought about how and whom on earth you are going to sell to or sign up if there is nobody for you to speak to?

So if you observe what you are actually doing right now and all the time as a network marketer, you are searching left and right, high and low, constantly looking everywhere just to find someone to camp around a coffee table at a coffee shop just to talk to. This is doing the business in the traditional way.

As a traditional network marketer since the age of 17, I have been doing the same old thing the hard way everyday. This includes distributing flyers, cold-calling, talking to some random people while having break at a cafe, camping around at the coffee tables and other offline promoting activities.

I literally tried everything that I can think of just to get leads for me to share and talk to, but it seems like more than 90% are those who either rejected or somehow conveniently became missing-in-action all of the sudden. Sound familiar?

What makes it more challenging is that all of my leads are limited to the places that I can reach. I mean, I plan to meet with them, so they at least need to be in the same country as me.

This caused me to think that it is really a waste of time and effort, as the time and effort that I have put in do not come back with much conversion. Furthermore, the target audience is already limited, and now, they even need to be local.

If you are facing these kinds of challenges as well, I am here to tell you that it's normal. All these, including brainstorming and the trial-and-error, are all part of the process. This is how you learn and grow.

I'm not saying the tasks I just listed are wrong. In fact, they are one of the many ways, and I am not here to put down anyone who is doing it in the traditional way. All I'm here to do is to tell you that there is a much better way, at least for me and for people who are similarly looking for other alternatives.

After sticking with all sorts of offline strategies for 5 years, everything changed in early 2016, when I came across one thing called "Internet Marketing." At the time, I quickly recognized how powerful it can be, but I didn't truly understand its full potential until I got to know Simon Leung.

Simon really opened up my eyes and allowed me to see how he made use of the Internet to generate leads. His strategies and skills really blew me away and it was totally opposite of what I had been doing all along to generate leads.

Why do I say this? Well, as I mentioned, I am used to doing my network marketing business the traditional way. This traditional way needed me to invest around six to seven hours a day, and I actually got less than ten leads doing that.

However, by using his way as described in this chapter, I only invested one to two hours a day in the beginning, and was actually able to generate up to 30 to

50 leads! Isn't that amazing for an online marketing beginner?

To me, I really think so. I was completely amazed at what Internet marketing can do, and out of so many platforms, Facebook is one of my favorite platforms that I personally use. Applying the strategies that I have learned really made my life much easier.

One of my successful experiences after the mentorship of Simon Leung is that I followed every single instruction and strategy that he taught, which is to consistently do Facebook postings in groups, create teaser campaigns in my own Page, giving away free things and doing Facebook ads.

I have also learned that every little thing that you post on Facebook is crucial. Each post has to mean something and is considered as a stepping-stone to your next post, the post after that, and of course, ultimately your goal.

The results? I not only started to generate leads, but actual income that got me USD sales within just the 3rd week into the business. That was simply crazy!

Can you imagine you are doing something that takes you as few as one to two hours per day, and you don't even have to step out of your door and do the talk yourself, and you can still get leads and sales online?

As a traditional network marketer working so

much more with fewer results, this is something I would used to consider as just some kind of myth. That is, until the moment that I personally tasted it. It's no myth.

Well, based on my true story and results, this online method is proven to work, and it has the potential of getting leads all around the world and even sales from out of nowhere.

Give it a try. I am sure it will definitely give you personal freedom, which is the combination of financial freedom, time freedom and location freedom that everyone desires. I no longer do it the traditional way anymore, and neither should you.

CHAPTER CONTRIBUTION #2

Lead Generation Through Posting On Own Facebook Timeline, Page and Groups, Along With Types Of Teaser Content And Target Market To Attract More Attention

Contributor: Pudji Sugianto
Team Leader, Speaker, Elite Member

I use Facebook all the time, but I had never thought of doing business with it. That changed after I joined this business, because I realized that Facebook is a powerful tool to get leads. The best part is I can do this even though I live in Indonesia, and even better is that it can be free!

From the previous section in this chapter, you learned how we could use Facebook ads as a paid lead generator. Here, I will talk more about free strategies previously discussed as a lead generator based on my own experience.

In the next chapter, you will learn more about the things that we give away to our prospects. One of these things is an online sharing session in an app called WeChat.

To promote this sharing, I posted on my own Facebook timeline. This WeChat sharing was our campaign to warm up any cold leads that do not know us or anything about it.

And yes, by only making a Facebook post on my own timeline, I actually did get cold leads that were interested for the WeChat sharing.

In the post, I stated that my mentor, who is a world-renowned Internet entrepreneur and professional speaker all the way from the U.S.A., would be giving a rare free Internet marketing session online. This means that we could listen to this at home, office or anywhere else. No need to bother to come to a venue and no need to fight through the crazy Jakarta traffic.

I also stressed that this online session will be giving 100% pure content to his existing students and partners, and because I am one of them, I can invite up to 5 friends only who are interested in Internet marketing to join this online session for free.

It's a very good offering, isn't it? I think it is.

To my surprise, an old childhood friend commented on the post, and said that his brother who lives in Surabaya, someone I not seen or talked to for more than 20 years, is interested in Internet marketing.

He asked me how to join this session.

To cut a long story short, I got in touch with his brother, and invited him to join the online session. Impressed with the online session, he actually flew over from Surabaya to attend to our live event in Jakarta, which was the event that was promoted on the WeChat session. More information about promoting live events through WeChat sessions will be discussed later on inside this book.

After some minor discussion, he ended up joining us, and he is my business partner now. You see, I was able to successfully replicate the results taught by my mentor, and it's only a simple Facebook post on my own timeline. The best part is that it's free. Yet, it's powerful enough to get leads and even business partners.

To get these kinds of results, rule number 1 is that you have to make sure your Facebook post is honest. Don't post some hypey false claims and screenshots of unrealistic results just to get leads. You don't want to do that because we are not scammers. Network marketing is a legitimate business.

To increase the conversion rate, you also need to regularly post teaser content in your timeline before you post the actual event or product launch or whatever you want to promote.

The teasers hint that something exciting is coming, but be careful not to reveal too much too early. That way, people become intrigued and begin to wonder what we have up our sleeves.

You also have to put your own picture on your Facebook profile. Don't put a picture of your pet or cartoon character such as Donald Duck or Mickey Mouse, or flowers and trees or anything like that. The reason is people like to deal with people they can trust. Real people, not a faceless person.

You also need to think who your target market is, and if you are using Facebook ads, you can easily set your target audience. How about with Facebook timeline post? The audience of your Facebook timeline posts is usually your friends and your friends' friends, which can be very diverse.

In this particular case, you have to clearly indicate in your content posts exactly what your target niche happens to be. For example, on my above sharing, I clearly indicated my target audience is people who are interested in Internet marketing.

The above strategy can also be applied to Facebook groups. The advantage to post on Facebook groups is you will have a bigger audience, as there are countless groups that have tens of thousands and even hundreds of thousands of members.

Therefore, your posts can reach more people. You can also choose which groups are the most relevant to your target niche.

With Facebook groups, you can also grow your network the legitimate way. You can make new friends with people in the Facebook groups, add them as your Facebook friends, make conversations with them, and build rapport with them.

Eventually, the time will be right for you to introduce the business opportunity to them directly through Facebook chat, which are all strategies that you can learn in this book.

That's how you can use Facebook as a lead generation tool. I do it all the time, and it works wonders for me, and it can do the same for you.

CHAPTER CONTRIBUTION #3

Newbie Gets Initial Facebook Ads Rejected And Zero Clicks After Approval, But Increases Conversion Rates Dramatically After Minor Tweaks Advised By Mentors

Contributor: Jian Ming
Team Speaker, Elite Member

When the team organizes events, they are considered important. The first time I attended Simon Leung's live event on the topic of Internet marketing, I not only learned a ton during this session, but I was so deeply moved and inspired that I wished more people would also get to know about this sharing, and attend. I knew it would change their lives, just like it changed mine.

As a marketing newbie, my initial thought is that since I managed a few Facebook Pages before, I should also be able to run Facebook ads. It seemed easy.

The reality is that despite how simple it appears, there are lots of strategies behind it. At my first attempt in promoting the next event on Facebook, my ads were disapproved.

Yes, my entire campaign was not approved, I thought:

"What? Why are my ad not approved? What guidelines did I not follow?"

As I only had limited time, I quickly created another ad with some small tweaks, then I submitted again. The process was the same: submit, review and wait (again).

When I came back to the ads again, I saw the red symbol again, indicating that the ad was once again not approved.

"What? Again?" I thought, getting more frustrated.

I was disappointed, stressed and felt panic all at the same time from the rejection messages sent by Facebook.

This is how I felt: "I am giving you money, Facebook! Why don't you want it? Why are you rejecting me again and again? Since, you don't want it, then I also don't want to give it to you."

I was very frustrated and I just gave up at that instant.

A few days later, which was about 3 days before Simon's live event, I felt it was wrong that I just gave up like that. A lot of people would miss the opportunity to learn from Simon. A lot of people would not get the benefit that I was getting. A lot of people would miss the chance just because they did not know about the event, and it would be all because of me.

With that in mind, I tried again. I tweaked some part of my ad and clicked submit again. In the third attempt, nothing changed, and the result was the same.

"What happened? What did I do wrong? What should I do?"

I wanted to ask my coach, but I didn't dare, as I was so late to do my part. I was given my link almost a month ago, but I had only just started to take action.

I could only think of asking another resource, and hopefully, I would get answer. I "Googled" my issue, and the search results showed some information and I revamped my whole ad.

Finally, I was APPROVED! I was so happy. I started to check my Facebook frequently to know the ad's performance. I was very excited with the result.

Throughout the duration of around 2.5 days, I only spent RM 66.87 (about $17 USD) and I had 14,871 people reached and 763 website clicks! I was so surprised with the result. With 763 clicks, I can definitely get people to register for the Simon's session.

Finally, on Simon's event day, I purposely went there early to help out and checked my show-up rate results with the team. With my ads reaching 14,871 people and 763 website clicks, I thought that if I can even get 1%, that would mean 7.63 people registered.

To my very surprise, I was told that I had ZERO registered. Yes, zero! I didn't get anyone to register. I was completely shocked and my mind went blank.

After awhile, people started to enter the room to register themselves to Simon's session. Although I helped to usher in the participants with a smile, deep down, I felt frustrated and angry, as I didn't bring anyone in.

After some downtime, I finally decided to invite my coach out for a one-to-one session. From just one session over a cup of coffee, I managed to clear lots of my doubts and set a clear direction and target for the next few months.

With the coaching support, I decided to give it another try. I again created a Facebook ad to promote the next session. With the right guidance, my ad was approved at the first attempt. I was so happy when it was approved.

I met with my coach again, and he showed me that I had 57 clicks to the event page, but this time, I actually had 5 registered. That's around a 10% conversion rate!

My coach then said to me: "I know you can do it!

You had good results. Keep it up!" I was so happy to hear that.

Through the experience and mentorship from my coach, I would like to share the below steps:

- Set your objective of your campaign/ad
- Know your audience. Set the correct audience is that relevant to what you are promoting
- Create relevant ads with related pictures and write up
- Monitor and tweak your ads
- Calculate your conversion rate
- Review your ads and improve

That's it! Always tweak, monitor and improve your ads. But first, just start. Once you do it, everything will fall into place.

CHAPTER FOUR
Build Your Business... By Giving Away Free Gifts!

*****

Nope, we are not going to leave anything to the imagination. Right here, right now, I am letting the cat out of the bag by revealing the main secret to making money online is, in fact, by giving away free gifts.

Whether you realize it or not, this is an aged old secret used by some of the top marketers as well as the most famous brands in the world. Even for big retail companies, I'm sure you would notice that many would give away free samples of their products from time to time.

In the world of online marketing, this is the proven model that has made the successful Internet marketers millions of dollars with their cyberspace businesses.

The best part? It costs them nothing because if they choose the correct business model and use the right tools, giving away free things could potentially cost them nothing.

Because there is a way to use this model to sell or promote pretty much anything you want online, there is no reason why it would not work on a network marketing business. In fact, it does work, with flying colors.

I have personally crafted multiple online campaigns that do just that. Allow me to explain what we created.

You see, with any network marketing business, there are traditionally two angles in which a company can be promoted:

1) The products and services
2) The business opportunity

Let's go ahead and examine what you can give away for each of these angles.

*****

When you are working on the product angle, the concept is easy. Simply do what the salespeople at your favorite department stores do: Give away free samples.

For instance, if your product happens to be

available in packets, you can choose to ship off one or two of them. If they are pills, you may also choose to send your prospects one to three days worth of supplies.

Alternatively, if you have access to decision makers within the company, you may suggest to them that they create trial-sized products for this free trial campaign.

In this case, the costs associated with this promotion may include the products, packaging and shipping. As a general rule of thumb for actual products, it is recommended that while the product is advertised as free, the buyer is ultimately responsible for the shipping costs.

You can then use the shipping cost paid by the customer to subsidize for at least part of the overall expenses. If you do proceed with this idea, it is recommended that you do not overcharge the shipping cost to the point where it covers your own cost for the product, as this would be deceiving the customer into thinking the product was free, when in actuality, they are overpaying for the shipping cost which fully covers the price.

Always keep in mind that the longevity of your business ultimately boils down to how ethical you are in your business practices. It is not worth it to lose a potential long-term customer or partner by saving a few bucks, selling out yourself and your own integrity in the process.

The downside to this angle is that you would always need to keep stock and maintain orders. You would also need to pack products and make frequent runs to the post office, and may even need to deal with customer support.

For most network marketers, they would prefer to simply let the company's own staff handle all of that, which is why the majority would not choose this option. After all, some of the main benefits of a home-based business is that you do not need to keep inventory or deal with customers, and creating an environment where you are now personally responsible for handling your customers' needs basically defeats the purpose.

Although, if there is a way for you to cooperate with the company and have them handle all the orders directly from their warehouse, then this would be the most ideal option for a hassle-free campaign.

If you can somehow get it to work without much trouble on your end, then the free trial product offer would surely prove to be a profitable campaign for you.

This is assuming, of course, that the product is as quality as it claims, and customers will be convinced to come back time and time again to re-purchase the items.

On a marketing standpoint, nothing sells better

than free, and a quality product available at no cost is simply the best way to hook in long-term customers to your products.

*****

Along the same lines of giving away free products, when you are approaching the business on the opportunity angle where you are looking for those who are interested to become partners, this is where more options are available to you.

Oftentimes, depending on the option that you choose, you may even be able to give away free things that do not cost you anything to deliver. This is all possible with the beauty of the Internet and everything that automated technology has to offer.

However, free does not necessarily mean no investment, as a great deal of your own time may be required in order for you to set everything up. Alternatively, you can even invest in software, tools or more technically savvy experts to help you with this process.

When operating in the business angle, what you may want to do is to give away free presentations or even education. The beauty of the Internet is that the traditional words that you speak can now be replaced with text on a webpage, and presentations you would normally need to give over and over again can be replaced by a single video that you upload online.

For example, if you want to provide free education, you can give it away in the form of a free report that users will download. The file would instantly be downloaded onto their computer, typically at zero cost to you, and they would instantly be able to view it directly from their PC, laptop or smartphone device.

The "free report" strategy has been around for a very long time, and it is usually extremely effective because those who visit your webpage are more often than not looking for the type of content that you are offering.

As mentioned, since nothing sells better than free, conversions tend to be high for something like a complimentary report which does not cost the user anything to access.

Another educational gift that you can give away can be an audio training, such as ones that are done through online platforms, such as Whatsapp, WeChat or Facebook, just to name a few.

Because of the popularity of these platforms among various countries, free training sessions on these apps typically draw a good number of interest, as well. All you need to do is to spend an hour or so of your time to give a live audio training with your voice as your way to bring educational value to them.

With the Internet, you also have the option to give away free education in the form of videos. The videos may be pre-recorded if it happens to be the same presentation and you do not want to say the same thing over and over again, which means you can upload the completed videos onto video sharing websites like YouTube.

If you prefer to do them live so you can have an audience with whom you can interact and answer questions, Google Hangouts and Skype also allow you to switch between your webcam and your own computer screen so you can choose what you want the users to see.

The ultimate goal for giving away education is to deliver value to anyone who has interacted with you, thus increasing your own overall credibility and making them trust you more, which will increase the chances of them joining you once you finally present the business opportunity to them.

Remember: At this stage, you are still in the relationship-building process. Your main goal is to bring value to your end users so they will get to know you, like you and trust you.

In the business world, there is nothing like

showering your potential prospects with free gifts of education and knowledge to start building a strong business relationship with you.

Since for most of these gifts, they typically do not cost you much money outside of the equipment you already have, software you need anyway and a bit of time to prepare and record, this is definitely a worthwhile investment for you to ultimately build an automated business.

What do you after your prospects attend your online training sessions or watched your videos?

Well, friends, it is now time to officially introduce them to your opportunity by inviting them to the next stage of your online marketing plan that, by the way, is also free for them.

CHAPTER CONTRIBUTION #1

Giving Away Free Products To One Prospect Which Convinced Him To Not Only Sign Up, But To Upgrade To A Higher Package And Ultimately Invested In A Few Extra Packages, And Giving Away Another Free Product To Another Two Prospects Who Also Signed Up, Then Returning The Following Week To Sign Up Another Package

Contributor: Ming Liang
Protégé, Lead Mentor, Team Leader, Speaker, Trainer, Elite Coach

Selling is hard work and I'm really not a fan, so ever since the beginning, I already decided that I won't be doing any selling. Instead, I share what I love and do what I like. What do I like to do?

I like to give away free gifts whenever I'm in a good mood.

If I meet nice people I like, I may give away even more free gifts. Nobody refuses anything that is FREE. In fact, 99% of human beings can't resist the word

FREE at all. In their minds, they will instantly and almost automatically accept anything that is offered to them for free.

Unfortunately, in business, free things are limited. It may be free to them, but it's not free to you, which means it is counting towards your promotional costs.

However, understand this. The reason you are giving away free gifts is simply because you want to use these gifts to grab more attention and ultimately increase your sales volume.

So, how can you make sure your free gift strategy is effective? The way I usually do it is by setting rules for those who wish to claim their free gifts.

Firstly, set a time limit. That's because you want to test the level of sincerity a person has, and see whether he is black horse material or not.

Secondly, have you met my requirements? Usually, there is no room for negotiation. If they do not accept it, I will take away by the end of the day or after I leave the room.

This is because I only make the offer once I feel that I want to work with that person, and he or she has the potential to be my black horse.

If a person tells me he wants to follow me to build and grow the business together with me, then he may be genuine. However, if he cannot commit at that moment, or he has this reason or that reason not to sign up, then I will immediately know that he is not black horse material.

This is simply because a black horse doesn't have any handle breaks to pull. A black horse usually knows what he wants and knows what he needs to do in order to get it. Only the real black horse deserves the rewards, don't you think so?

The type of free gifts to give away usually depends on what kind of situations you wish to control. The most common one is at the big events, where the event organizer will give away lucky draws to make the crowd stay.

For websites, you can give away some relevant training, videos, e-books, reports or any small trial packs for free to gain your subscribers.

In the network marketing business, if you want to improve your sales, I have tried and tested several effective tips regarding free gifts that can help you boost your sales.

Tip #1: You can create a special products package for an indecisive prospect whenever he is trying to figure out which package to take.

This usually will lead him to take the bigger

package. That's because if he cannot afford it, he wouldn't be considering the bigger package in the first place.

Therefore, if he is considering it, this means he has the room to go for it. Usually, this could be your black horse, so you can consider offering a bigger free gift to attract him.

Based from our experience, multiple customers whom we gave a free box of our health product or beauty product not only joined us at a higher package, but they ultimately invested in another two extra packages to begin their journeys with us.

Tip #2: Give away something that most people desire to have, but won't be able to get it even if they have money.

Sometimes, people are willing to take out their wallet when they see this kind of free gift. This effective marketing strategy has been in practice since a long time ago, especially over the counter at certain direct sales stores.

From our experience, our customers even return to us the following week and wanted to buy another package in order to claim another gift.

Tip #3: Give away your products as Christmas presents, Season's Greeting gifts, Year End-Appreciation Hamper, and Get Well Soon or Valentine's gifts.

During any of these special occasions, they are the best chances for you to introduce your relatives, friends and business associates, customers and suppliers to your fabulous products.

This method has been proven personally by me to work because our gift recipients from other countries eventually became our business partners, and they are expanding themselves in their own countries now.

Tip #4: Give away a trial pack of products, which is a small-sized one-time use trial pack.

I suggest giving away this trial pack after a strong introduction about this product, and give it out only when you see some sparks from your prospect's eyes.

That's because through our experience, many people only like to accept free samples, but they never really appreciate it. Some have forgotten where they've placed it, while others completely disregarded that you even gave it to them in the first place.

So, the effective way is to introduce the product

first, and if they really like it, only then would I take the trial pack out, open the packaging, and help to apply it on them.

Let them see the results immediately and close the deal on the spot. From our experience, this method gives us very high closing rates and return purchases. This method can be performed at anywhere and anytime.

Tip #5: Free Facial Trial (half face), strictly by invitation only.

When you invite your guests to some kind of facial party or event, they already know that you are going to introduce them to your products and may even try them on their faces.

To ensure this method works, the host must edify the demonstrator or speaker to the invitees before they arrive to the venue. As well, this method usually works only if you have very good and effective products. And if you do, it would work extremely well.

These are the 5 common free gifts promotional strategies that we use in our businesses all the time. They all work because the products speak for themselves, and they even sell themselves. All I need to do is share.

CHAPTER CONTRIBUTION #2
■■

Proof That Giving Away Free Educational Gifts Works From A Partner Who Accepted A Free Mini-Seminar And Signed Up, Then Also Gave Away Free Gifts Like WeChat Sessions And Live Events To Sign Up New Partners

Contributor: Sam Eng
Team Leader, Speaker, Elite Member

Is "FREE" a good thing?

While many people expect that free gifts are usually worth nothing more than just a gimmick, I actually experienced the opposite. Free things changed my life significantly!

It all started with a WhatsApp message from my wife on a nice evening in September of 2015. It was an invitation to a free online business seminar. I rushed to the seminar at the very last hour before the seminar.

Unbelievably, I was introduced by Simon Leung to a free automated online marketing system, which included a free sales funnel, free promotional live seminar, and even free coaching from two world-class Internet gurus.

So, is "FREE" a good thing? It is not just good. It is GREAT!

It's so great that I have created my own marketing philosophy for it, one that I have named "The Great Free Things," or "T.G.F.T" for short.

Is that the end of it?

Well, it is not the end. Great things should be shared, right? "T.G.F.T" is a sharing business. I started sharing it using the free Internet marketing system that I got, along with the free training and coaching from the gurus. My online business flies high!

Two months later, I got my first "out-of-nowhere" sale by sharing free things via the Internet. My first partner came on board and joined me without me even being there, and I received my first income in USD.

When I first started this "T.G.F.T" online business, I literally did not know how to promote anything online. I knew nothing about Facebook, as my timeline is like an abandoned land.

My mentor advised me to start off with what I'm good at, which is WeChat, since I have many friends in WeChat whom I can share the "T.G.F.T" business instantly.

Via WeChat, I grew my business even more with

one partner after another joining me. My new partners started to share "T.G.F.T" virally, and WeChat soon became one of my favorite platforms that helped to accelerate my business.

WeChat is not just a chatting app. It is actually an app that combines three functionalities in one: "Chat" + "Social Network" + "Payment Gateway."

The "Chat" function is just as other chatting app, which connects us with our contacts for conversation and communication. However, the outstanding functionalities are actually the "Social Network" and "Payment Gateway".

Because the payment functionality currently remains a local feature for the China market, I will not elaborate much about that. Rather, I will talk more about the "Social Network" functionality that truly became the soul of my "T.G.F.T" business.

Like Facebook, WeChat communication starts off with the contacts we have added as WeChat friends. My WeChat friends are my leads as well as leads generated elsewhere for my online business. Because they are my leads, I share "T.G.F.T" with them.

WeChat limits the number of friends possible in one account, so it is good that we select WeChat friends wisely. We need to add quality and relevant WeChat friends who can help us share the "T.G.F.T" business.

There are several ways to add friends in WeChat. Here are the most effective ways that I would recommend.

First, join WeChat groups on relevant topics and start adding members in the groups as friends. Introduce yourselves and know their background, keep in touch, and share knowledge and info, just like making friends offline.

Once you have built up rapport and trust with them, your sharing will be effective and they will become intrigued by your ideas. From there, you will create their interest to know more about your business. Most of the time, they may even help you share "T.G.F.T" with their own friends.

Yes, that's right! They become your lead generators! Isn't that great?

Secondly, WeChat has a virtual space for us to post our ideas, wisdom quotes and pictures. Similar to the Facebook timeline. This is called "Moments" on the WeChat app.

WeChat Moments allows us to share our valuable information and knowledge with our friends. From here, we build our authority and influence to the WeChat community. Once we gain the authority and influence, our "T.G.F.T" business will spread virally.

Isn't it awesome? Amazingly, it is all FREE!

By the way, WeChat does not just chat, it talks! My mentor conducts free talks in WeChat via voice messages to share free Internet marketing knowledge. At the end, we also give out free seats to live seminars that introduce the "T.G.F.T" online business.

By simply giving away a FREE WeChat talk, I eventually got my business partners on board through autopilot thanks to the variety of systems. Within 6 months after I encountered "T.G.F.T," I am now an Elite leader in my group, a trained live seminar speaker, and even contribute back to the team by launching my own WeChat talks.

Yes, I also conduct WeChat talks, sharing "T.G.F.T" to many friends who are interested to grow online business with the free automated online marketing system.

I started by getting "T.G.F.T" and today, I continue to share it online to listeners all around the world via WeChat, not to mention offline through live seminars.

I shall call this the "circulation of good deeds!"

CHAPTER CONTRIBUTION #3

Malaysian Doctor Who Broke Through The Mold Of Traditional Mindset Towards Home-Based Businesses And Accepted A Free Report Online, Which Led To Eventually Signing Up As A Partner Without Having Met His Mentor Or Knowing His Sponsor's Identity

Contributor: Dr. Fazley Rahman
Team Leader, Speaker, Elite Member

"If your business is not on the Internet, then your business will be out of business." – Bill Gates

As a medical doctor & lecturer in Kuala Lumpur, Malaysia, I have been working as a government servant for many years and received monthly pay-cheques.

With a medical degree, a stable professional career and a good salary, I had never thought of having financial difficulties in my life. But in reality, the world has changed.

In short, there was a mismatch between my monthly income and commitment. If this can happen to someone like me, what about other people who are less fortunate than me?

I had no other options than to find at least one source of income, but how? Where? What can I do? Is there anything outside there that is suitable for a busy man like me? These are the questions that had been lingering in my mind for a long time.

I started to attend courses, workshops, seminars and reading books on business, investment and Internet marketing. I learned many new things and concepts that I had never been taught in school or even in university. I began to realize the importance of creating multiple sources of passive income for a better living.

I had subscribed to many mailing lists in Internet marketing. Out of all the emails and newsletters, there was one that captured my attention the most. This is the one opportunity that led me to my eventual partnership with world-famous Internet entrepreneur and mentor, Mr. Simon Leung.

After reviewing the contents meticulously for several times and compared it with all the other courses I had enrolled in before, the salesletter that explained this partnership, mentorship and online system seriously impressed me.

How to ensure that your salesletter captures the intentions of your readers? Simply create the best, unique and most complete package they have ever seen. This was exactly what I saw, and I'm sure many more before me, as well as after me.

Ever since I started to learn about Internet marketing and online business, I honestly had never seen a better package. Why?

Simply put, it combines a complete Internet marketing funnel system, and it's even ready-made by world-renowned Internet marketing gurus. It also includes six weeks of Internet marketing coaching online, advanced mentoring by world-class experts and high quality products that are endorsed by recognized authorities.

Plus, due to the flexibility of the system, it is VERY suitable for 9-to-5 office workers or government servants like myself to generate extra income passively without interfering with our daily jobs in office. Wow!

Many other Internet courses I attended in the past focused on only one or certain parts of the funnel system. This means that I have to attend several other courses or buy multiple products or services from many different experts just to create a complete Internet marketing funnel system for my product.

Just imagine how much that will cost me and how much time I would need to spend to create a proper Internet marketing system with very little or almost zero knowledge in this niche! And one more thing, even if I created a complete marketing system myself, I still wouldn't have any of my own products to sell.

With everything all in one place, that's why I was so confident that this is THE ONE I have been looking for. This is THE ONE for me.

I decided to sign up, even though I had never met or talked to my mentor in person prior to that day! Anyone else who truly understands the value of this package would have done exactly what I did. Trust me!

So far, the training is superb and above my expectation. My mentor, Mr. Simon Leung, is a very charismatic, but down to earth guy. Together with the team mentors, especially Simon's Protégés, they have set a very high standard for his students to follow.

Much more importantly, these guys walk their talk. And since I joined this group, I have met with many new like-minded friends who are all highly motivated and very passionate about this opportunity. With the tremendous support, who wouldn't be?

This business has definitely improved my knowledge on Facebook and Google marketing strategies, and the importance of leadership and teamwork. With ecommerce, there is NO LIMIT to how much I can earn since I don't have to trade time for money (the traditional way). That's because I can leverage on other people's expertise, time and other factors.

With this system, it is now not impossible for me to retire 10 years earlier, something that was almost impossible to me before. In addition, from a medical background with zero knowledge in online marketing, my knowledge and skill in this subject have also improved significantly.

As a bonus, my public speaking skill has also improved exponentially, credit to my mentor, the multiple International award-winning speaker, Simon Leung. This is truly a invest one and get thousands in value package!

I will continue to share and spread this opportunity to many more people to help them. I'd wish someone had told me about this many years ago. But still, better late than never!

"I am not a product of my circumstances. I am a product of my decisions." – Stephen Covey

In conclusion, to join this ecommerce opportunity is undoubtedly one of the best decisions I have ever made in my entire life. My goal is that sharing this experience can confirm to you that an effective online system works, and there will be many more people like me who will sign up with you as long as you do a good job putting together the best package you have to offer.

CHAPTER FIVE
Introduce The Business Opportunity For The First Time

*****

In the previous chapter, we discussed strategies that are designed for cold leads, AKA people you do not know who also do not know you. For this reason, we take them through a relationship-building educational funnel where the goal is for them to know you, like you and trust you as they read your reports or watch your videos.

Well, I'm sure you are wondering at this point: What happens after that?

Eventually, the relationship-building process stops and we need to get down to business. This is when you finally introduce the business opportunity to your prospects for the very first time.

While there are three online methods that I will be sharing here, take note that there is a fourth way which, even though it is an offline method, has proven to be the single best converting method of all time based on my own experience.

With that said, it is up to you whether or not you would want to implement it with your team in your own marketing. However, among all the unconventional methods I have used throughout the years, this strategy has proven to be able to sign up the most members in a single shot time and time again.

For this reason, I feel that I would be amiss if I did not include it in, and even though it is technically an offline method, the combination of having invited the prospects there from a premiere online strategy makes this a hybrid technique worth its weight in gold as long as you put it into good use.

It is important to note that when you show your prospects the business presentation videos, they should be warm leads that you have already spoken with and are expecting to learn more about the business opportunity directly.

*****

In the traditional world of network marketing, one

of the most successful methods of signing up new partners on board is the one-on-one personal selling strategy. As a matter of fact, this was the only way the business was built for a very long time.

While it is arguably one of the most loathed methods because it requires both you and your prospects to patiently sit through potentially hours of a presentation conducted over company booklets or a tablet device, it cannot be denied that this is the method that enrolls the most partners.

For the presenters, it is particularly dreadful because there is always a fear of rejection, as well as potential questions the prospect may ask which they do not know the answers to. They also need to practice, make sure they say the correct things, and hope that they do not mess up.

Even worse, if the prospect ultimately does not sign up, there is probably no feeling in the world that would make the presenter feel as depressed as that point in time.

The truth is, personal selling may not be suitable for everyone. It requires skills, patience and the right personality to make it effective. If you are shy, introverted or simply do not speak with fluent confidence, then forget about it.

Because of this, it makes it almost impossible for

somebody with this type of personality to be successful in this business. That is, until now.

Since we already touched on the topic of online videos, and personal selling is the traditionally-proven way of signing up new partners, here's an idea: Why not combine both?

That's right. Thanks to the power of technology, it is now possible for you to create a video that simulates an actual personal selling experience. If you're not comfortable doing the video yourself, you can ask a confident member of your team to record it, after which, all your members can have access.

Now, there are probably countless ways that you can do this, but I will describe two ways that makes the most sense to me and have proven to work well for me in the past.

The first way is to simply record the computer screen and talk through the slides of your normal business presentation. To do this, you will need to have a soft copy of the presentation on your computer, which may be in PDF, Word, PowerPoint or any other file format that can be easily viewed.

You will also need to have some kind of screen recording software. Depending on how long you intend to have the videos and what kind of computer you have (Mac, Windows or Linux), there are different options available.

For example, one option is a screen recorder called Jing, which has a free version that records up to one minute each. Then, there are also other software programs that offer limited time free trials, such as Camtasia and Screenflow. To use the full features of each application, you will eventually need to purchase a license from the creators.

In any case, choose the software of your choice, and use it to record your screen while you or a member of your team simply talk while you are going through the presentation. This presentation should mimic the actual personal sales experience as if the prospects were there live, including the disclosement of the total investment at the end of the video.

The other way is to record yourself or a member of your team while sitting at a table with your presentation, and making sure that the presenter is actually inside the shot of the camera. The presenter will then look into the camera and speak, while showing portions from the actual slides of the opportunity presentation.

This method makes the viewer feel as if you are actually in front of them and presenting to them over coffee. If you are more technically advanced, you can edit the video to transition between the presenter and screenshots of the presentation, which fills up the whole screen, similar to professionally recorded presentations from live seminars with speakers on stage.

*****

Along the same lines of using videos, a variation of the business opportunity video in a personal selling format is recording a full-length presentation that also contains educational content.

Think of it like a real presentation a professional speaker would make at a live seminar. If you have attended live events in the past where they are not network marketing opportunity presentations, but rather speakers whose intention is to make platform sales, you will notice that their sessions typically run between 90 minutes to, sometimes, two hours or longer.

This is because in addition to presenting their course or business opportunity, which is typically introduced at the end of the presentation, the speaker also spends a great deal of time building rapport with the audience.

Just like us, the speakers want the crowd to know them, like them, and trust them. With nothing else except the stage, they aim to build relationship with the audience by educating and entertaining them during their short time together.

Well, in this type of video, which would ideally in a live webinar format, your presentation should be the exact same way. This means that your video should aim to be 90 minutes to two hours, along with educational and entertaining content designed to build rapport with your audience.

As with the speaker in a traditional stage presentation, you will then introduce the business opportunity towards the end of your video. This is where you will explain the company, its products, potential earnings and total investment required to join you on the team.

Of course, it goes without saying that since you want your viewer to join your team, you should disclose some of the benefits of working with you as opposed to somebody else.

I mean, it makes sense, right? You are not the only one promoting this company. It's not as if you can give them some kind of discount, since everyone makes the same investment.

Then, why you? Is it because you have special training? Key experts on your team? Specialized systems that no other teams in the world have?

You must be absolutely clear on this because otherwise, you are not giving the viewers any real reason to join you as opposed to another friend who may also be chasing them to sign up at the same time.

*****

Not comfortable to speak on camera or record your own voice? Don't know how to prepare the slides for the visual presentation? Can't find anyone on your team who can help?

Well, what if I were to tell you that it is also possible to take advantage of online technology without creating slides, playing with video software or even opening your mouth?

Yes, this is indeed possible. In fact, this method could very likely be the most popular form of making sales of any kind in online marketing.

Let me ask you this. Have you ever ran across a website that actually is not really a website at all, meaning that there are no navigational menus or any clickable links?

When you scroll down the page, all you see are long blocks of text where the author of this webpage simply wrote an extremely long article that talks about the product or opportunity, along with lots of other content like stories, graphics, images, photos, videos and even some testimonials.

Sometimes, this goes on what seems like forever, simply because the amount of copy is so long. In reality, many of these webpages can go as long as 15 to 20 pages, sometimes even more.

Have you seen webpages like these, and thought to yourself that this is the most annoying kind of website you have to go through, and it is not until the very end where you will finally find the "Buy Now" button to see how much the product actually costs?

If you find this kind of website annoying, I have some good news for you. This is exactly the kind of website you need ☺

In the Internet Marketing world, this type of webpage is called a "salespage," or a "salesletter." As frustrating as it is for many readers to scroll through countless pages of sales copy, the salesletter is actually proven to be the highest converting type of website of all time.

So much so, that a professional copywriter may charge upwards of $10,000 or more for a single copywriting project. There are also some famous copywriters I know who currently charge $1000 per page, which averages about $15,000 to $25,000 per project, sometimes even more.

Making a salesletter convert does not only rely on its length. Copywriting is a skill on its own, and there are lots of technical, psychological and other sales elements involved.

Nonetheless, when done correctly, a salesletter is your ticket to making sales from "out of nowhere" without ever having to talk to a single person.

When your salespage is completed and on a live website, simply send the URL link to your prospects and ask them to read through the whole thing. Since the salespage is already equipped with a "buy" button, and ideally instructions on how to sign up, the prospects should be able to sign up themselves once they have read through the whole salesletter.

Not only has this been a proven method for over 10 years in the Internet Marketing world, resulting in millions of dollars getting made in as little as 24 hours, but we have also proven that this works also with network marketing.

When you put it all together, you will realize that having an effective salesletter that describes the whole business and even sells for you is one of the best ways to automate your sales process, all without talking to a single person.

*****

As mentioned previously, while videos and

salesletters are effective ways to sign up new partners all online, the best unconventional method to convert new partners without doing personal selling is undoubtedly leveraging on the energy and power of live events.

Whether in a small group setting or a seminar room, when combined with a trained speaker who has had sufficient practice with a high-converting sales presentation, the conversions can go through the roof.

Even though the use of live seminars typically work best with warm leads, just like any other strategy, it is still possible to convert completely cold leads if the speaker does a good job warming up the crowd and following the strategies to build rapport with the audience.

Remember the kind of presentation I was talking about earlier, where the speaker does a live 90-minute to two-hour presentation that ultimately introduces the business opportunity? It needs to be that kind of presentation.

Similar to the salesletter, the 90-minute presentation is yet another time-tested proven strategy that converts. In fact, many experts will tell you that this kind of sales presentation is actually the spoken version of a salesletter.

Although when you add your own stories,

combined with real emotions and on-stage charisma, a good speaker can bring the salesletter to life and make the presentation a thousand times more powerful, resulting in even more sales.

Moreover, live presentations also have the power to command a higher investment compared to any online strategies, simply because the real sense of urgency is there, along with real social proof that can be witnessed by the audience.

Again, when done the right way of using online methods to generate the leads and warming them up, then subsequently inviting them to an offline event, this is the ultimate hybrid that will skyrocket sales for any business.

CHAPTER CONTRIBUTION #1
■■■

Stay-At-Home Mom Presents The Business Opportunity To Overseas Strangers She Has Never Met And Successfully Attracts Them To Become Her Business Partners... All Online!

Contributor: Danyelle Tan
Team Leader, Speaker, Elite Member

Would you believe me if I told you that you can enroll new business partners without you meeting them, calling them or even knowing them at all?

Most traditional network marketers would not believe that because they were taught to do exactly the above. Some people who are desperate even pester their family and friends until they run away from them.

As a result, while many would like to enjoy the lucrative income of a network marketing venture, they will choose to stay away from this business.

I am a stay-at-home mom in Penang, Malaysia. When I started my business, my daughter was just one year old. As a busy new mom, it was very inconvenient for me to present the business opportunity via the traditional network marketing method.

So, I used one very simple tool to help me build my business without having to meet anyone. In fact, this simple tool enabled me to tap into the cold market. This simple tool is the sales letter.

By the way, in this business, it is the hardest to invite your own family and friends to come on board with you. The much easier way to grow your business is to get into the cold market.

"But how? As a stay-at-home parent, it's just impossible for me to network with strangers in any networking events." Yes, I know. I totally understand where are you coming from. But, relax. Let me share my experience with you and you will see the light.

From Chapter Two and Chapter Three of this book, you know that you can get prospects easily by using Facebook alone. If you do not have a Facebook account, you better register one for yourself. It's free.

I consistently share some interesting teaser posts on my Facebook profile and some relevant Facebook groups. I usually set the privacy of all these posts to "Public." This is how I tap into the cold market to attract prospects to send me a personal message with the intention to know more about my business opportunity.

Now, do you realize that with this simple attraction

marketing strategy, you no longer need to cold call your family and friends or pester them, like what the traditional network marketers do?

My next step is to build rapport with them by asking questions using FORM methodology. "F" stands for family. "O" stands for occupation. "R" stands for recreation. "M" stands for message. If they continue to show more interest during the chat, I will then send the salesletter to them and let it do its job.

Basically, the salesletter acts as an online sales person. Hence, it is vital to have a compelling salesletter that pulls the prospects or customers right into it and see clearly the benefits that are presented against the very reasonable investment required.

One thing I like the most about our free online business tools is the effective salesletter written by a world-class Internet marketer. The sales letter is attached with my unique sales tracking link that I can use to promote my business.

All I need to do is to send the salesletter link to my prospects, including those from overseas, because there is no geographical limit on the Internet. The salesletter will do all the online selling for me, and I typically don't have to explain anything.

Let me share with you one example on how I got a business partner easily from another country by just using the salesletter.

One day, by making a simple Facebook post, I received a personal Facebook message from another full-time working mom in Doha, Qatar. I've never spoken to her before, and she wanted to know more about the business opportunity.

So I just built rapport with her as discussed before, and when the time was right, I sent the salesletter link to her. Later, as I was visiting my parents, she expressed interest in coming on board with us, but had a few questions.

After she clarified with me on a few things via online chat, she signed up in Qatar directly through the salesletter while I was here in Malaysia, spending time with my parents. After she became my business partner, we only communicated via online until I finally met her in person about three to four months later when she visited Malaysia on a family trip.

In fact, 90% of my business partners were initially strangers, and I only met them in person many months after they became my business partners. Now, we all are good friends.

As an introvert and a stay-at-home mom, I really love the way we do this network marketing business online because not only do my current friends and family don't need to run away from me, I actually have more friends because they are interested in my business opportunity.

Don't you think this is a much more relaxed and effective way of building the business?

CHAPTER CONTRIBUTION #2
■■■

Overseas Prospect Tunes In For A Live Webinar And Is Immediately Convinced To Sign Up By The Automated Global Power Witnessed In Action

Contributor: Hendry Lee
Team Leader, Speaker, Elite Member

A few months before the writing of this story, I was still recovering from the economic crisis that had hit my Indonesia-based business due to weakened market in recent years.

One important lesson this taught me is that now, I should always have a plan B in mind in case the main business fails. To me, the ultimate plan is to build a business that allows me to enjoy a stream of passive income.

As a re-born businessman who has been through ups and downs, I have always been motivated by new business opportunities, which is now the Internet era. So eventually, I began to learn Internet marketing.

After taking classes after classes, I improved my

knowledge on the subject, but they did not motivate me to start taking any action. Maybe the classes were not convincing enough, or maybe I just hadn't found the right business model yet.

One day, I saw an Internet marketing event being promoted on my Facebook's news feed. It was an actual live event that would feature Internet marketing gurus coming to my hometown, which meant I didn't need to travel, so I did the most logical thing: I registered and attended the preview.

It was a brainstorming seminar presented by two world-class Internet marketing gurus, including my current mentor, Simon Leung. Because I had other things to attend to, I could not stay until the seminar was over, and I had to leave before I had the chance to talk to the team.

After things settled down and I finally had some time at home, I felt regret that I could not stay longer at the seminar. Hoping to find a way to get more information on what I missed, my intuition led me to Simon Leung's website.

There, I was lucky to find out he would soon be conducting a live webinar online. I quickly registered for the very next session, and watched the webinar presented by him live while I was at home in Indonesia, while he was in another country.

For some people like myself, I believe that they would prefer an online webinar experience. To me, English is not my native language, so reading requires more effort and energy, while watching video is more enjoyable because I can just sit back and watch the show without much thinking.

During the webinar presentation itself, Simon successfully explained the core value and benefits to the topic that I was looking for, which was learning more about online marketing.

More importantly, I was amazed how he could campaign his education and business opportunities, all the while able to communicate with more people globally in less time than a live seminar, and actually able to put together such great results, all from only an online webinar.

In total, I had spent 2 hours of my busy day to join the online experience, but it was worth it because I gained valuable information and developed a level of trust with him which helped push me over to the line of signing up to the project he was offering in the webinar.

There are many things I have learned from Simon's strategy using webinar to present business opportunities or products. One of them is you should always consider the audience you reach and make sure the topic is relevant to them.

Your audience is not only giving you their email address, but also their precious time to learn from you. As a result, it is always better to focus on being educational rather than salesy.

Another important aspect is building trust with the audience, which means you need to show that you are the expert on the topic, something that Simon has demonstrated simply by the quality of his content and the way he confidently presented it.

By doing this, the probability of buying will increase. In any business or opportunity, it goes without saying that people will only buy the product from those they trust. That's why quality content is important, which convinced me to trust him.

At the end of the presentation, the final call-to-action would also be more powerful if you are able to give bonuses after bonuses. For simply joining the business at the same investment that everyone makes when joining the opportunity, Simon distinguished himself from the rest by doing a great job over-delivering on the bonuses to make sure his prospects see the value in the offer.

In the end, I believe that video is for everyone. I mean, we all enjoy TV or YouTube, right? Nowadays, magazines and newspapers are struggling to survive, while at the same time, online videos are booming.

Smart marketers know how to tackle on the hottest trends, and you should figure out what you need to do to leverage your business with online webinar videos. This is not only for generating leads, but also increasing the probability in sales when it is used properly.

I truly believe the power of video marketing is the future business strategy we all should consider. Numbers don't lie, as active users and new videos are increasing day by day.

That said, online webinar is one of the best ways to gain trust with your audiences, especially to a global market. Simon Leung's webinar presentation already proves that webinars work from an overseas partner who signed up right after attending a webinar on his website. That partner is me.

CHAPTER CONTRIBUTION #3
■■

Consultant Who Made A Living In The Training Business Searches And Finds His Next Challenge After He Himself Attends A Live Seminar, And Now Strives To Also Become A Speaker In This Business

Contributor: Nik Fuaad
Team Speaker, Elite Member

The one person who got me on my Internet marketing journey is none other than Simon Leung himself. I was captivated by his stellar oratory performance at his seminar the night that I attended, where I was completely mesmerized for the whole 3-hour duration.

Coincidentally I spent the best part of my professional career having to present to clients. I am a civil engineer by profession, and have worked with consultants, developers and contractors. Currently, I am the MD of a consultancy outfit that has a JV with Universiti Sains Malaysia (USM).

Now that I am 57 years old at the time of this writing, retirement plan looms. I could just carry on as a consultant indefinitely, but this is not a dream profession.

I have financial freedom, but not time freedom. Worst is the "client is always right" mindset that was built-in from early on, meaning no personal freedom and location freedom.

Always lacking is the quality time to do the things that I really love, which includes spending more time with my wife in our empty nest (now that all of our 5 boys have left home), playing golf all day and, best of all, do nothing at all.

I have been looking for something I could do after retirement, something that can earn much more with less work, preferably with little investment and low risk.

This Internet marketing thing is actually not as simple as I first thought, but certainly nothing could be more difficult than what I have gone through in the consulting business.

After only a few months under the mentorship of Simon Leung and his team, and having attended several training sessions, I eventually have a greater insight into the workings of the Internet marketing business.

I have now full confidence in Simon's business model, and am sure now that this would be my last venture. I also need the challenge to keep my youth adrenalin flowing. This would probably be my final professional endeavor.

Simon has picked me to be one of the speakers for our team. I have to admit that deep down inside me, this is something I have been looking for all along... to do something that I am comfortable and good at, or at least I think I am.

It's not really for the money, but just for the fun of it. If you like what you are doing, then it's not work. Better still if you can also help other people to benefit, as well.

It is a privilege to finally learn the art of public speaking from the world's best. I have always advocated that if you want to learn something, learn from the best teacher available.

Simon has taught us the insider secrets to public speaking, and more specifically, how to influence the audience to make a positive sales decision. In addition to being some sort of entertainer as well in order not to bore the crowd, we need also to give some information regarding the business.

Public speaking will be a breeze if you have the passion for it. More important is we must be sincere and believe in what we are presenting. Then, only genuine emotions will bloom. Once the crowd is with you, the game is yours.

Although, this is easier said than done.

A little bit about my past, I was actually born a stammer. As far back as I can remember, I hated teachers who asked students to read aloud passages from textbooks.

Surprisingly, this was the norm in the sixties and seventies. You cannot imagine the consistent nightmare I went through in junior school.

The nightmare continued into high school until this one Bahasa Malaysia lady teacher taught me the techniques of effective speaking. I remembered her telling me that despite my stammer, I have a strong character and positive mindset. It was she who gave me the confidence.

Months of personal coaching from her transformed me, a stammer into someone who not only could read passages in class flawlessly, but could also speak in public with ease and confidence. I went on to represent my school in inter-boarding school debate competitions, and we were once the champion.

One important item that Simon always emphasized is to have the correct mindset. Early on in life, I have subscribed to this philosophy. There are many stammers who never got rid of this debilitating handicap. Without the correct mindset, I would not have overcome mine. Where would I be now?

CHAPTER SIX
If At First You Don't Succeed...
*****

In the perfect world, everyone who stumbles across your website would be interested in your offer. They would then submit their names and contact details to access your gift, be presented with your business opportunity presentation, and hastily sign up to be your partner without a second thought.

Unfortunately, the universe is not perfect, and in the real world, real people have questions, problems and other issues they need to consider prior to making such a decision. This, of course, is very understandable, since it is a business model that may not be suitable for everybody.

What does this mean for you? Does it mean that you should give up on them and let them go their separate ways?

Absolutely not. In fact, statistics show that those who have already been presented with the business opportunity and did not sign up have a high chance to come back and inquire about the partnership again.

At that point, your odds of converting them into a business partner have infinitely increased. With this fact in mind, then it obviously makes sense for us to be more proactive in our business, and actually take the first step to make the effort to contact them as soon as we can.

In this business, it is called the follow-up process. When you follow up with potential partners who did not sign up the first time around, you are demonstrating your sincerity to help them succeed, or to become more healthy, beautiful, or whatever your company's products may be.

Following up with your potential partners and customers is a strategy that can take up a variety of different forms. If you are comfortable talking to people, you can speak with them over the phone or even meet up with them face-to-face.

On the other hand, if you prefer to follow up with your potential partners online instead, this has also been proven to be an effective way of closing the sale. In this day and age of technology, it may even be a preferred method of communication by most people. When people are more comfortable, your sales also increase.

*****

Staying true to my Internet marketing background, the most popular style of follow-up is email marketing. When communicating over email, neither the sender nor recipient would feel any form of intrusion.

Emails are personal enough to get the message across, yet still impersonal enough a communication method to keep both parties from feeling uncomfortable if the answer is not so favorable.

That said, there is no denying that email marketing simply works. It is time-tested and proven by some of the most successful online marketers in the world who build wildly profitable businesses and attributed it all to email marketing.

Not only is it profitable just to average Internet marketers, but the way you know that it works extremely well is by observing some of the biggest brands in the world today that use emails to communicate with their customers every single day.

For example, if you have ever registered or made transactions on global online retail stores, I'm sure you are constantly receiving emails from them, as am I.

If you are a registered user on websites such as Amazon, Groupon, Ebay, Expedia, Agoda, Facebook or YouTube, just to name a few, I bet you receive so many emails from them that your mind begins to ignore those messages every time you see one in your inbox.

The reason these big companies email their users and customers is that email marketing is a proven marketing campaign that will bring people back to their sites time and time again. When you use this for your own business, it will have the same affect, as long as you do it right.

How do you do it right? Well, unless you are a globally recognized brand like the companies I have listed above, you do not want to do what they are doing.

Sure, it works great for them, but that is because they are household names with a loyal customer base who may even be excited to see emails from them on a daily basis.

You, on the other hand, may still need to spend more time building relationships with your prospects before they would feel the same way about hearing from you. This means that you need to continue to send them educational value to the point where they will finally feel like they know, trust and like you.

After receiving their initial information, do not send them product offers or introduce the business right away. Remember, you need to deliver value to them, so you should focus on that.

Avoid emailing them too often. Maybe every few days, send them an article or video about something interesting and relevant on the topic in which they expressed interest.

When the time is right and you have already presented the business opportunity to them, follow up with more value-added content alongside a brief message that asks them if they have any questions about the presentation.

Initiate the conversation and attract a response, but do not be pushy. This would only turn people off, as it would make yourself appear overly desperate.

Instead, continue to send them more bonuses, or even offer to help them with whatever business or life challenges they may have. Here and there, softly sneak in a mention of the business again, or at least something associated with the business.

For example, you may mention that you might not be actively emailing them because you'll be preparing for a live training from your mentor this weekend.

Or, you can excitedly share some video testimonials from team members, saying that you are so proud of them for their first "out of nowhere" sale.

In any case, these emails are designed for you to

give your potential partners gentle nudges about the opportunity without being overly aggressive.

You should openly and directly discuss the details of the program only after the potential partner has expressly asked you to tell them more. Think of it as opening your mouth to speak only after you have explicitly attained permission.

When you are finally in the discussion phase of your follow up process, make sure you proceed with patience, as most people may tend to ask questions that you feel are already answered.

Keep in mind that not everyone has the same attention span, and while some may be able to collect information at a rapid pace, others may require the same details to be repeated several times prior to effectively absorbing them.

Whatever the case, exercising patience is crucial at this stage of the follow up process. After all, if you are already here, then chances are, you are a very short stop away from making the final close. Be patient and considerate, and your sincerity will show in your communication, resulting in a successful signup.

*****

When the follow-up process starts to become more

serious, you may discover that it is not always possible to complete the signup over email. Oftentimes, the potential partner may prefer to have a private message chat via FB Messenger, Whatsapp, WeChat, LINE, KakaoTalk or other similar chat programs.

The use of these chat programs are typically straight-forward and non-invasive, as they allow both users to communicate without talking, which is ideal for somebody who does not want to speak during this process.

However, there is always an advantage to speaking, as it may be an easier method of communication for all parties involved to better understand each other.

If this is the case, the good news is that with the same chat programs, there are options for you to send voice messages and make free calls online. While this would then require both parties to use their voices to communicate, this is still a form of follow up that is conducted online.

Another alternative if you are both on computers or smartphones is to use voice or video chat programs, such as Google Hangouts, Skype, Facebook Messenger, Whatsapp or WeChat. With these platforms, you can easily make free peer-to-peer calls and even turn on your webcam if you decide to.

Similar to following up over email, take note to exercise with patience if using this method. Especially if you are using voice or video where your emotions and reactions will instantly show, you do not want to give off the impression that you are frustrated with your potential partner.

Whatever the case, keep in mind to act as professional as possible because at the end of the day, everyone has a choice which team they would want to join, and they will always choose to join people whom they know, like and trust, and feel the mutual respect returned back to them.

*****

Through it all, while even the follow-up process is possible to do online with the aforementioned methods, this is another example of when a certain strategy should also be considered for offline. The reason is that when you are in the final stages of closing a sale, nothing can demonstrate more sincerity from you as taking the time to sit down with your potential partner.

After a series of online interactions with your prospect, there is no better time than now to finally make the personal connection with your potential partner and have some actual real human contact.

Besides, after you become partners, you will need to meet up often to plan how to take over the world together.

With even more patience and understanding than ever before, prepare to meet up your potential partner and discuss the future of your partnership together.

What makes this face-to-face meeting different from traditional ones is the fact that you indeed have an online system to speak of, which would make it so much easier for you to get somebody excited about partnering with you.

Rather than meeting up with prospects and telling them that they would need to do the same thing as everyone else, describe all your online and unconventional methods in detail. Talk about the free gifts, email marketing, salesletters, seminars and anything else you may have set up.

Because most people will be attracted to the fact that this project can be done online, even though this is a personal face-to-face meeting in the traditional form of network marketing, having the Internet marketing platforms associated with your team is a big enough distinction that will convince any prospect decide to work with you as opposed to your competitors.

CHAPTER CONTRIBUTION #1

Partner Who Has Used All The Follow Up Methods (Email, FB, PM, WeChat, Whatsapp, SMS, Phone, Meet Up) To Sign Up Prospects From All Presentation Methods (WeChat, Events, Meet Ups) Reveals How It Is Done

Contributor: William Cheong
Protégé, Lead Mentor, Team Leader, Speaker, Trainer, Elite Coach

How do I follow up with my leads that have created new sign ups time and time again?

Yes, this works even on cold leads, and has gotten me new partners from "out of nowhere" on many occasions. The way that I do it is by following this blueprint, which I am about to share with you.

Create attention: Without attention, no follow up would be considered a successful follow up. If your prospects or those in your email list do not respond to you, this means you have done something wrong or bored them to the max already.

Now, how do I attract their attention by either sending them emails, Facebook messages, WhatsApp or WeChat? Actually, this is no mystery, as I simply base my communication on a few key criteria that works on us as humans.

My most effective strategy is through curiosity, as most people are curious with anything that they don't know. For example, you can PM or email them with something that goes something like this:

"Hei XXX, I know you have left early yesterday, but did you know that there are a few people who earned their first commission this morning by simply following the S.T.E.P.?"

The word "S.T.E.P." will trigger their curiosity, because instead of "step," you are using "S.T.E.P." as if there is something hidden behind these 4 letters. As a result, they will start to think, what is this "S.T.E.P." all about? What is the secret behind these 4 alphabets that makes it easy to get commissions?

With this, they would itch to know more. Eventually, they would answer your call or message, and maybe even request that you come out and talk more with them so they can understand more from you.

Now, you have successfully initiated a conversation or meet up without forcing them to come out. Isn't that cool?

Another strategy that I commonly use is leveraging on people's greediness. How can you do that? This is simply just giving away more bonuses, or even downsell your products if you are desperate for sales.

Here is another example for you to follow:

"I know yesterday you have heard about the 'Exclusive Bonus.' It is very attractive, as most of the attendees agreed. Although, did you know that there is one more hidden bonus that is worth $3,000 USD, but the speaker actually did not announce it in the room? Basically, this bonus might help you to get your sales and make back your investment within as short as 1 week!"

What's the key phrase here? This is it: "One more hidden bonus worth 3,000USD." Another one would be "make back your investment" within a certain amount of time.

Now, most people would get attracted by the bonuses, as this psychology is just like when you go to the shopping mall. There, you would always be attracted to the sales that offer something like "buy 1 get 1 free," am I right?

For this reason, when you throw in extra bonuses for them, very seldom would they turn you down. Eventually, you may evoke certain conversations with them, as well. I would always leverage on this opportunity to invite them to come out and have a meet up to let them understand more about it.

Once they request for you to come out, this already means that they are open to a second chance for you to propose your business opportunity to them. If you are able to initiate these meet ups, your chances of closing your new partner will significantly increase.

The strategies mentioned above are what I always use to write the emails, as well as sending some PMs, or replying to chats. Or, if a meet up is not possible because of geography, schedule or any other reason, after capturing their attention is a good time for you to send them the online webinars or salesletters.

With all the results tabulated, usually those who answered your invitation to discuss more can get you as high as a 70% chance to close your new partner.

This is because they have already had time to think about it, which is the most common reason why most don't sign up right away. Since they already thought about it and agreed to talk with you more, you most likely will not experience the "I'll Think About It Syndrome" from them again.

In the end, the answer will simply be "Yes" or "No."

CHAPTER CONTRIBUTION #2

Team Member Shares Own Prospecting And Follow Up Strategies That Intrigues Her Prospects From Both The Business And Product Angles Resulting In Easy New Partner Sign Ups In Record Time

Contributor: Thiam Sok Kiang
Elite Member

Since I got into this network marketing business, I have learned a lot about prospecting and following up with leads from the training provided by the team. Besides getting good results, I have been enjoying the process very much.

The key message that I want to share is always be prepared to adapt to any situation or opportunities that may arise. Here are a few instances.

1. FROM "NO" TO "ON"

My first approach is to build my candidate's profile to match my prospect. This particular prospect is a retail operations and events trainer with good human networks and is very persuasive and convincing in her own right.

I told her that I am looking for partners who can be leaders, can do presentation, and have good networks. I then asked whether she could help me to find someone who matches these requirements.

Now, if that person were alert, she would think, "Hmm... I could fit into that role." This would pique her curiosity to find out more about what this business is all about.

To keep up with the suspense, I had to cut short the online chat by excusing myself on the pretext that I had something urgent to attend to. I believed she would come back to inquire more.

True enough, after 10 minutes, she replied asking me to switch to Google Hangouts as her hand phone battery was low. She was interested to learn more. I quickly obliged as I realized it was "now or never."

When I presented my business proposal, she was adamant that she is not the leader that I was looking for. So I quickly changed the topic towards the product angle, and casually talked about how we need to take care of our skin and our looks at our age.

I then followed up by sending her a video showing the application of one of our company's products, which is a cream that can remove eyebags and wrinkles in less than 2 minutes.

Unsurprisingly, she was in awe of the product. However, she then went on to check out our company's other products herself on YouTube, and was also impressed by another one, which also happens to be our next best-selling item.

My friend maintained that she was only interested in one of the products, but did not want to sign up. I tried to convince her, but she was steadfast in her refusal, "NO, NO, NO!"

She even wrote me a poem. This is what she wrote:

"SK, you are my true friend
I want to be truthful to you
I treasure our friendship
That's why I want to be frank with you
I joined many MLM all these years
I have never sold a thing
I won't do anything
I don't want to be another downline
I know myself
I can't sell
I will disappoint you
I don't want this to affect our friendship
I just want to buy products from you."

I was touched, but I had to think of a response quickly. At this juncture, I had to change my strategy and directed her to a lower cost package by comparing the price of one product against the package price that only costs a little more, but actually comes with that product and three other fantastic products.

My friend was quick to spot the bargain and happily responded with an emphatic "ON" and signed up. Amazingly, this process took me only 2 hours to close.

I find it remarkable, especially considering that I had not done any seeding on her before, and during the chat, we switched from Whatsapp to Google Hangouts, and then back to Whatsapp again with some intermissions in between.

After a week into using the products, she was so thankful for my recommendation, and hinting that she might want to look at the business plan again. I truly believe she can be a leader with lots of partners with the training provided, and not just being another downline that she is so dreaded about.

2. "BETTER THAN NOTHING"

The second approach was to identify the potential needs of the prospect. Another one of my prospects has been working very long hours and possibly needed something to perk her up.

I had a close look at her FB profile picture and noticed that she has rather big eye bags. I sent her the relevant product video via Whatsapp at early dawn, as I knew that many people would check their phones first thing in the morning once they open their eyes.

My instincts were proven right. Before she left for work, she dropped me a chat message asking about it. Because I did not get the chance to reply to her initial message, she sent me another one at lunch hour.

This time, I briefly explained about the product. I advised her that it only lasts about 8 hours and she remarked "hou koh mou," which is Cantonese for "better than nothing."

However, at the time, my prospect insisted that she just wanted the product only. As a result, I cut the chat short, did not pursue further and continued with my own daily routines.

In the evening, while she was driving home around 10pm after work, she called me and started to pour out her pain in work. She was contemplating a backup plan.

During this call, she became very interested in the business after I explained in greater deal what we were doing and our strategies behind it. The actual phone call only took us about half an hour before she signed up.

3. BEAUTY AND THE BIZ-NESS

My third approach was to zoom in on what the prospect is known to be interested in. This prospect is always on the lookout for beauty products. I did not intend to approach her from the business angle because she is already doing well financially.

For this prospect, I had not spoken to her for the last 6 months, so I started with some greeting chats, and then only casually asked about her beauty routines. The door of opportunity almost immediately opened when she started complaining about the skin care products she was using previously.

I sent her the beauty product video. She fell in love with it instantly and asked how she can get it. She also asked me about the other skin care products, and questioned about their effectiveness.

Based on her request for more information, I sent over the "Before" and "After" pictures of myself using the skin care series. She saw the dramatic change in my skin, from the dull complexion to the radiant-looking one, and that was all it took for her to be immediately convinced.

My prospect was very impressed with the products and signed up right away. Furthermore, the added bonus is that she is very interested to do the business. That really caught me by surprise!

In most cases, I worked around with my prospects' needs, be it from the business or products angle. As marketers, we need to be sensitive to their problems, listen to their grouses and the pain they are experiencing physically or mentally, suggesting some solutions to them, but not insisting that yours are necessarily the best.

When sensing the door has opened, only then would I proceed to recommend suitable packages to them, explaining the options, and letting them decide according to their financial abilities.

Based on my experience, I also need to be flexible with my approach during the entire process, and especially the follow-ups. Anything can happen, and it can turn out to be the exact opposite of what I originally expected.

Before you embark on the conversations, it is also important to keep all the important products demonstration videos and even your own testimonial pictures handy, because specific questions may come up, or your prospect may request them at anytime.

For those like me, since I do most of my follow-ups on the go, it is especially important to have them ready in your smartphone. You will never know, maybe during the break from your busy-ness, instead of aimlessly surfing the net, you could be building your leads and closing the deals at the very next instant!

4. NAME DROPPING

In my final real-life example, I will talk about my long time air conditioner technician who is now my old friend. From time to time, he may be on the look out for business opportunities.

I have not seen him for quite a long while, but one day, I happened to bump into him while he was doing some work at my friend's house. I briefly chatted with him and shared with him about my business.

During the course of the conversation, he was quite interested. Then, due to time constraints, we could not finish the chat, as he had to rush off for other services.

When I followed up with him a few days later, he has already "gone cold" and did not respond to my messages. This is not out of the ordinary in our business, as people get busy, become distracted or simply lose interest after letting the idea sit for too long.

Then one day, I decided to send him some greetings via WeChat just to spark a simple and casual conversation with him. This time, he replied, and I started to chat with him, asking about his family and his business.

He started to talk about how the rising cost has affected his net income and the heavy responsibilities to provide for his three young kids. As this topic became a natural transition to our previous discussion, he mentioned the reason for his unresponsiveness is that his wife was quite skeptical about network marketing due to his past failures in MLM.

At this point, I knew I had to pull some tricks up my sleeve. I remembered my mentor had advised that whenever possible, we need to implement "leverage," whether it would be on something, or someone.

With little time to react, I quickly mentioned about how my mentor, Simon Leung, has guided me and led me into achieving success in my business. I asked him to Google "Simon Leung" to find out more about my mentor for himself.

To my surprise, the name-dropping worked like a charm! Not long after my suggestion to him, he messaged me back that he is impressed and wants to register for the upcoming preview.

In this case, I simply leveraged on the brute strength of Simon Leung's credentials. When you can find yourself a mentor with similar authority, use this name-dropping strategy to effectively impress your prospects enough to turn them around from someone who is skeptical to someone who wants to learn more.

CHAPTER CONTRIBUTION #3

University Student Proves Her Skeptical Friends All Wrong After They Told Her She Couldn't Do It By Consistently Making USD Income In A Business Easily Through The Power Of Following Up Online And Offline

Contributor: Janice Tan
Team Leader, Speaker, Elite Member

When I first started this business one year ago, most of my friends doubted me.

"Are you sure?"
"This won't make you money."
"You're wasting time. Focus on your studies."
"You shouldn't do this. You will soon have a professional qualification. Get a job in a big company after you graduate!"
"Just enjoy your university life!"

What did I do when others doubted?

"Just prove it to them!" – I told myself. I did exactly that, and this was how I started my home business in a small town near Ipoh in Malaysia.

What's my secret to proving it to them? Well, it's no secret at all. I simply learned that it is important to "follow up" with our customers and prospects, and that was exactly what I did.

When I'm selling to my targeted prospects, most of them usually would not give me a positive response right away, and it's likely that I would need to follow up a few times, or maybe even more, to make the sale and achieve my goals.

Therefore, I have a database to record all my lead information that contains their names, phone numbers, email addresses, etc. If their contact information changes, I make it a point to keep the database updated to make it easy to follow up with them.

Personally, I feel that the "trust" between prospects and me is the key factor to build up this business. Also, we should not oversell to them because this might annoy our prospects.

Normally, I would make the effort to spend time to keep contact with them online via Facebook, WeChat, Whatsapp and other social media platforms. From time to time, I may also allocate time to meet up with them to build the relationship.

Most of the time, I would start the conversation casually with greetings and, whenever it's suitable, I would "chat" with them on other casual topics, such as things you would discuss with friends. During the conversation, I would try to talk about some related topics to know about their current situation and their needs.

At the right moment, I would then let them know exactly how I can help them to find their solutions and fulfill their needs. At the same time, I would mention about what I'm doing and present myself as a valuable resource.

I would also ask if they have any questions about what we have discussed during our last conversation and share updates with them if there are any new information, promotions and events.

After a few rounds of following up in the right and sincere way, especially when I'm showing an honest desire to build an ongoing relationship with them, they would often be appreciative and I could easily close the sale in the end.

Sometimes, it may require a longer period of time to follow up and build the relationship with them. However, do not give up. When we continue to do this consistently, we are one step closer to our goals!

Following up can be a very simple and effective

way to close sales. At the same time, I have also created valuable friendships with my prospects, too.

This is how I started to build up my business from zero, and you know what? It's very effective. Today, I'm able to get new customers quite often, and it is easy for me.

After a while, I began to show my achievements to my friends, the same ones who had doubted me. At first, they were surprised, too. However, some of them actually said to me, "You won't be able to maintain that performance" or "You're not going to build it much further than that."

Well, I am happy to report that I proved them wrong again. That's because besides successfully continuing to sign up new customers with the same strategies, I'm also able to make repeat sales from my old customers, too!

How? Again, I follow up with them after the sales. I drop each of them a message or an email to collect their reviews, keep contact and update them about the latest promotions and results from time to time.

You may think that it's time consuming to do all this hard work. If this is you, then you really need to ask yourself: What are the end results of putting in all this hard work? Goals will not be reached on their own.

In addition, all my customers are very satisfied

with the before and after sales services! As a result (and reward to me), they are not only making repeat orders, but also making referrals to their friends and family, too!

I remember the customer who once told me, "Sorry, I'm not interested about this at all." This person even ignored my first few follow up messages, but finally made a purchase with me after a few months of consistent follow up.

After that, this person actually told me, "Thanks, Janice! You are a very nice person. I'm happy to know you! I appreciate your caring and kindness and that's the reason I decided to purchase from you! Hope we can keep contact always! (Followed by a *kiss* emotion)."

This was one of the most touching messages I have ever received from a stranger that I have never met before, and now, she's my online friend. I would say that besides wealth, the creation of new friendships is something very valuable that I have earned from my business!

Today, I'm consistently making income from my business. I proved those who doubted me wrong. I have good relationships with my customers, and I'm able to gain wealth, happiness and satisfaction all at the same time.

If someone were to ask me about my opinion of the key factor to making consistent sales in a business, I would share the exact same thing to them that I shared with you here.

Follow up, and if it doesn't work, keep following up until it does. You will be rewarded in ways you never thought were possible before.

CHAPTER SEVEN
Lead Your Team To Network Marketing Success
*****

After your new partner signs up, you may think that is the end. "I did it!" You might say to yourself. While this may be true in any other business, in network marketing, this is only the beginning.

You see, traditional businesses may base their revenues on one-time sales. After they sell a certain product or complete a service, the merchant gets paid, and that is the end of it.

In network marketing, even though you do make a commission on each new partner sign up, the real money comes from the results your partners are then able to achieve. For this reason, you must be a leader.

The truth is that anybody can make money. With

the right mindset, attitude and work ethics, anyone can be taught to succeed. That is purely a personal thing.

However, if you have the passion to help others and the drive to build success together, that, my friends, that is most definitely a leadership thing.

This means that once you have signed up a new partner, it is now your personal responsibility to help this person succeed. In fact, if you have the right attitude, you will put in your best efforts to help anyone whether or not they are directly on your team.

The beauty of this network marketing business is that once you put on your leadership hat to help others become successful, you will, in turn, become even more successful.

Network marketing is one of those rare business models where your passion for helping others will directly have a positive impact in your own bank account. The more money your team members make, the more you also make.

Therefore, do not ever think that your task is complete the moment you close your new partner. Your responsibility is ongoing until every single one of your partners have completely maxed out on commissions based on your company's compensation plan.

For this reason, it is crucial for you to begin planning on how to take your team members to the top.

As everyone works in a team, the goal is for everyone to become successful together.

*****

Maintaining the theme of running your network marketing business online, you are obviously able to deliver any previously prepared offline content on the Internet using technology that already exists, all ready for you and your team to use.

For example, my favorite way of communicating with all my team members from around the world is through a private Facebook Group designed to support them. Obviously, only active partners are allowed inside, and it is used as a way to upkeep any important updates and announcements.

My leaders and I use this to provide motivation to the team, as well as to make important announcements regarding upcoming trainings, live events or any new strategies they can use to promote the business. It is a very convenient platform that allows instant communication to everyone on the team at once.

Facebook Groups allows admins to make unlimited posts in the group, and they can post as frequently as they like. It even has the capability to "pin" important posts to the top of the page so all the crucial information, instructions and resources are always in view. This is especially useful for posts that welcome new team members and shows them how to get started, which can include resources and links to other important posts.

As the admin, you are also allowed to make other members admins, which means that as soon as members are promoted into a leadership position, they now also have the capability to make posts, approve new members and contribute to leading the team.

Another way to provide even more instant support to the team is to add all the members into a Facebook Messenger chat group. With the entire team on chat, it makes it easier for instant communication, rather than making a post in the group and waiting for everyone to reply.

This is especially effective for anything urgent or otherwise in need of immediate attention. It is also a good platform for team members to ask support or product questions, which everyone can read and instantly reply to.

Like I always say to my own team, constant and consistent communication is crucial to ensuring that your team stays motivated and action-oriented. If nothing happens for too long, we run the risk of other things popping up in their lives that distract them from the business, and may result in the ultimate dismissal of more and more members from the group.

Discipline is also important, as members will need to learn to follow instructions and take requested actions in a timely manner. They need to be as active as possible, which could be as simple as "liking" all the posts, or creating open-ended content that encourages additional interaction through comments.

Any time members begin to show signs of drifting away, such as not interacting in the posts or maybe not even reading them, this should be taken seriously as it may be an indication that they are no longer interested in the business. Sure, it could mean that they were simply busy or had different things going on in their lives, but we don't want to risk it.

As a leader, do what you can to control or salvage any potential damage to the team before it becomes too late, resulting in a relationship that can no longer be saved. Overall moral and positivity is a must in order for the team to continue to grow.

*****

Similar to the new partner recruitment process, the same technology can be used to provide ongoing training to the team. As time goes on, there will be more demand for new educational content, and this is your chance to improve the moral of the team by providing value above and beyond their expectations.

For me personally, I like to use the Facebook Messenger voice message feature to provide regular trainings to the team. My leaders also help me out by conducting a good number of the trainings on a variety of topics, all of which are instantly accessible by team members regardless of whether they are on their smartphone, tablet or computer.

With Facebook Messenger, all the voice messages can also be downloaded. We take advantage of this feature by downloading all the previous trainings, join them into one file, and upload them onto an audio-sharing platform.

This technology allows us to archive the trainings for future members or anyone who may have missed the live sessions. We simply reserve a training archives section in the pinned post or Files tab, and anyone can access them by accessing the links.

Of course, training is not only restricted to audio format. If you are so inclined, you can use Facebook Live or programs like Google Hangouts and YouTube, which allow live streaming, so you can conduct live webinar or video trainings with visuals to your presentation slides to your worldwide team members right from the comfort of your own home.

Live video trainings are effective because in addition to providing content, you also have the option to make the virtual chatroom interactive. Team members can type in questions, or you can even open up the room for anyone to say anything at any time.

This makes the virtual room perfectly simulate an actual live training that would have been conducted in person, except everyone is sitting at home or wherever they happen to be while attending the training.

Similar to the audio trainings, these videos can also be recorded and saved into video files. The videos can then be uploaded onto Facebook or YouTube and viewable by existing or future partners at any time, forever archiving your training content so you would not have to do the same presentation more than once.

*****

Whenever possible, I always encourage teams to meet live. Of course, this may not be a possibility if team members are spread out around various cities, countries or if certain members are out of town, but if there are enough local members in certain geographical regions, regular meetups is an effective way to build and maintain team rapport.

Live meetups are able to achieve things that cannot be done online. The human touch is the most obvious example, but even when you sit around to discuss certain topics, the depth of the conversations can be so much more meaningful in person.

It also helps to build the relationship of team members on a personal level because they are now sharing meals or drinks together, and there are very few things in life that can have such a close connection with other people.

In addition to live meetups, you may also want to organize live trainings. When trainings are conducted live, members will be more prone to paying closer attention, asking better questions and producing better outcomes as a result.

Furthermore, live trainings have the capability to be more hands-on, step-by-step and interactive. You do want your team members to absorb the content, take action and produce results, right? From experience, I can tell you nothing outperforms a well-conducted live training session.

When all is said and done, our objective here is not only to educate the team, but also to build stronger relationships among them. Thus, when the time is right, this is when you should also consider organizing fun-filled team events.

That's because in an environment where the pressure to perform is non-existent and recreation takes its place, team members will be more open to be themselves, let their hair out and have some fun.

This can be achieved by planning any kind of activity, such as BBQ's, pizza parties, birthday celebrations, karaoke, or pretty much anything else that may include food and drinks.

Optionally, certain parties can even have a combination between fun and work. For example, you can open the events up for guests, and team members can bring any potential partners they may be talking to and introduce them to the team.

We have done events like this on multiple occasions, and some of my members have recorded as high as 100% conversion rate for prospects they invited to our team events.

If you want to bring even more value, pull some strings to invite your top mentors to attend the event. While building a personal relationship with the mentors, they can also do an impromptu sharing that will help everyone in attendance.

With these kinds of parties, team members may even become BFFs overnight, which can only improve their working relationship. I highly recommend it.

CHAPTER CONTRIBUTION #1
■■

Access To Online Training And Support Allows Overseas Partner To Communicate With Team And Consistent Motivation From Mentors Through Online Channels Contributed To The Never-Giving Up Mindset Despite Geographical Barriers

Contributor: Sungkono Surya Tjahyono
Team Leader, Speaker, Elite Member

I joined this group from a Jakarta, Indonesia event in November 2015, and like any other new experience, I was having difficulties in the beginning.

For starters, I had obstacles in terms of not knowing what to do, what is expected of me and how things are done within the group.

The fact that all the partners are spread out in different countries also plays a role in the dynamics of the group. I went through the orientation or the 'grinding' period to become accustomed to the culture of the team.

In this fast moving business, we can't afford to

plan out all the details and follow the conventional process. We have to act fast and adjust accordingly.

Fortunately, in this age, technology can help tremendously to bridge the geographical gap. Using the online resources that have been provided, I don't have to wait for my mentors to schedule a trip to Jakarta or for me to travel to them.

We have utilized numerous online resources, such as webinars for continuous training and sharing of the latest strategies, WhatsApp groups and Facebook messenger chatrooms for daily interactions and impromptu sharings, and Facebook groups for the latest news and team-wide progress status.

These readily available online resources have allowed me to stay in touch and communicate my concerns to the group. I've also been given access to a 6 weeks online training and a powerful Internet marketing system that has set me in motion on this new online journey.

Using those online resources, I have daily interactions with fellow partners and also directly with my mentors. Being in this group has given me not only access to actionable knowledge to run the business, but also a sense of belonging - in a tightly integrated and highly motivated group of people which I'd be honored to call my family.

Even though I can only connect with my mentors mostly through online methods, they have offered their support along with multiple opportunities for me to step up – not only to prove that I belong in this group, but also to help me achieve more than what I thought I was capable of.

As such, I have done many things for the first time and as a result of those actions, I have gained new knowledge and deeper appreciation for their guidance. The tasks they asked me to do were geared towards getting me out of my own comfort zone, to grow and realize my true potential.

These include recording multiple videos of myself sharing about my experiences, talking in front of the stage as a success story, initiate conversations with total strangers both offline and online.

As a matter of fact, three partners have even come on board through personal selling skills that I've learned from my mentors, where I had no experience prior to joining this group.

Due to the many negative reputations surrounding network marketing, I never imagined that I would be interested in one. However, being in this group has changed my perspective and opened my eyes to the many possibilities offered by network marketing. They have also shown me how to leverage on the already-created platform to build a business.

I believe that being in the right group plays a huge part in one's success and that's exactly what this group has done for me. They have helped to shape and reinforce my beliefs to achieve our success the correct way: with honesty and integrity. Without those two traits, there's almost no merit in doing what we are doing.

One of the reasons that pulled me in to join this group is their purpose, which is to help people to achieve their dreams. Having such a noble goal instills in me a deeper level of commitment and motivation to help realize it.

Hopefully, with the right attitude and positive actions, I can continue to inspire and lead by example, to make an impact in the lives of many people worldwide, as what my mentors have done.

So to build a good team, make sure you have an effective online support system to help motivate your team, just like what mine has done for me.

CHAPTER CONTRIBUTION #2

Lifetime Instant Access In Addition To Ongoing Live And Archived Online Training With Impromptu Sharing Creates An Environment Where Team Can Always Discuss, Inquire And Exchange Ideas Together

Contributor: Sue Tan
Team Leader, Elite Member

In today's tech-savvy world, it is pretty common to carry on conversations with people half way around the world, or to attend trainings without even having to leave your home.

The online training portal is the attraction and main decision factor for me to join this business. Thanks to the technology, I'm able to access the online training courses prepared by the experienced Internet entrepreneurs anywhere, anytime.

With this great platform, I often access the online trainings on the go by using my mobile device, which can be a smartphone or a tablet. I am able to go through the training modules at my own pace and execute the strategies learned right away.

When needed, I also can revisit the same training anytime I want. This gives me the opportunity to properly absorb all the information and skill sets that I wasn't able to the first time around before moving onto the next training module online.

Besides the online training portal, additional social channels were set up to allow our team members to learn and exchange ideas in order to gain a better understanding of business and execution plans.

What's better than learning from the experiences of fellow peers? Plenty of impromptu training and sharing, which are all conducted via various social channels, such as WeChat, Facebook group, Facebook messenger chat and Google Hangout.

It's always better to attend the trainings live so that we can post our questions to the presenter and get immediate answers, as well as being able to interact with fellow members who are also on the training at the same time as you.

However, as you can learn from this great team that I have, there will always be volunteers to record and compile the trainings, then update into an archived folder for those who are too busy to attend live and couldn't fit it into their schedules.

So, if any members missed the live trainings, they can still refer back to the archived folder and pick up the knowledge. Same goes to newly joined members. The archives make it never too late to be in this business and no one is left out.

In this business, I was not only given access to those scheduled and impromptu trainings, but I can also give a buzz to Lead Mentors for some personal consultation, too!

To me, I feel like I can't get this type of support from any business, and since it is a huge part of the success of my team members, this experience tells me that any team who can replicate the same online support system can also be successful.

CHAPTER CONTRIBUTION #3
■■

Why Online-Based Training Is Crucial To Achieve Success, Especially For Stay-At-Home Parents And Anyone Else In Similar Situations Who Need To Run A Global Business While Spending Time With Family

Contributor: Jasmine Tang
Team Leader, Elite Member

The dream of running a global business from the comfort of home while simultaneously taking care of my family is already a reality. Through the Internet, everyone has been given the opportunity to start global businesses that operate continuously for 365 days a year from anywhere in the world.

Yet, even though many businesses have been started because of this opportunity, many business owners have also failed due to the lack of proper training. While building a global business, I realized it was very important to be regularly updated with current trends, methods and updated with the latest technologies in order to achieve success.

Truth is, it's very possible that whatever I've learned and implemented into my business today could very well become irrelevant very quickly. It is inevitable that trends and technologies will come and go. That's just the way things go in this business.

In order for me to leverage on every opportunity that presents itself, I had to stay abreast of the latest information. Hence, it is of paramount importance to receive proper training at the right time.

However, it is a fact that there are many different trainings going on all the time, and as a full-time stay at home mom, I could not possibly attend all of them. Traditional trainings, such as seminars and expos, may be held in different states or countries with different time zones.

To make the effort to attend even half of these events would require that I neglect my family's needs at home. As a parent, it is my personal wish and responsibility to be physically present to give my children the necessary attention they require.

At the same time, my business also should not suffer due to my circumstances. Hence, it's important to see that online-based trainings are invaluable to those who are building a business from home while caring for family.

I consider myself very lucky because my mentors provided exactly that for us. Once their training lessons were made readily available online, I was able access it from anywhere in the world and at anytime as long as an Internet connection was available.

No longer would I have to miss out on learning about crucial bits of information or innovative ideas because of my preoccupation with family at home. As a parent, I was able to schedule my time to go through training when the children are in bed or being cared for by others.

I can even listen to training sessions through my mobile device while out of the house. Anyone on my team from different regions or time zones can receive the same exact training as I did through the Internet.

Online-based trainings can be in many forms. They could be PDF documents, pre-recorded tutorial videos, live webinars, web chat sessions, Facebook posts, and more. It just depends how creative you want to be and what kind of advanced technology you want to use.

Since all the content is online, I don't have to worry about distractions at home, since I am able to watch and re-watch the videos whenever I need to. As well, it is much easier for me to learn new techniques, take a refresher course, then implement and tweak whatever I have gained from the trainings immediately.

Although online trainings will not replace the same energy and atmosphere as when attending a live seminar in a crowded hall, it is still a major platform for myself as a stay-at-home parent to receive proper training for success! This way, I could build my business quickly and effectively while spending time with family.

In this day and age, online-based trainings are crucial to build a global business. I no longer have to worry about neglecting those who are important to me while working on growing this business. When you make online-based trainings readily available to you, it will be your best time to leverage on it!

CHAPTER EIGHT
Automating The Entire Process To Help You Sign Up New Partners From "Out Of Nowhere"

*****

Ah, business automation. That's really what you want, isn't it? This is the whole reason why you picked up this book in the first place, right?

After reading all the chapters, content and contribution pieces up to this point, are you beginning to think that this is possible, or perhaps becoming more and more improbable?

Upon closer observation of the hybrid and offline techniques, the answer is obvious that these solutions cannot be automated. I mean, how do you automate a live seminar? Or a face-to-face follow up session? Or a classroom training?

At the end of the night, this is a real business dealing with real people. There is clearly no way to automate the entire process. If you are serious about this business, you also wouldn't want to.

However, with the right technology, the good news is that most, if not all, of the online aspects can be automated, at least up until the completion of the sign up process. Once new partners join you, they must be introduced to the team and be provided with the resources to help them become successful.

In terms of training, supporting and leading your team to success, the only way to automate this would be to delegate the work to other leaders on your team. Although, I would say that a true leader will always be dedicated and personally involved in the growth and success of all their team members.

I mean, we are in the business of helping others, right? You cannot and should not disappear on your own team after making the initial sale, only to leave the hard work for your fellow leaders to do. This would simply be irresponsible on your part.

Now, back to the fun part. Supposedly, there is a way for you automate the process from the beginning to the end. How would that look like?

Well, take a look at this five-step blueprint of the "Internet Marketing Sales Funnel" to see if this is something you can build yourself. Who knows, maybe you will use it to create your own automated online system one day.

*****

STEP ONE: Find Something To Give Away For Free

Ok, first things first. The free gift is your "bait" to attract prospects to you. The quality of this free gift is important because it needs to be something that people want or need.

For me, I use free reports and video trainings. Both are effective because I am targeting people who would like to learn more about Internet marketing and wealth creation. When they are offered free educational content in this category, the free gifts are relevant to what they want.

While it is possible to search online for "private label rights" products that you can put your name on, give away and pass it off as if you are the author, the best way is actually to put in the work and write the free report yourself.

Yes, it would be more work, but keeping in mind that you will be known as the authority and leader of your team, you want to make sure you establish your credibility the right way, while upholding your integrity at the same time.

The report does not need to be very long. I have written free giveaway reports that are as short as 5 to 10 pages long. As long as the content delivers what was promised along with additional resources, the length of the product is not an issue.

For my videos, I simply create a PowerPoint presentation and, with the help of screen recording software, I would go through the slides and speak as if I were doing an actual presentation.

The software records my screen so the viewer can see the slide content, along with my voice as I go through the slides. This is an effective way to build credibility with your audience while showing off your presentation skills.

As with the report, there is no rule on how long the video should be. I have recorded free videos that go on for an hour, half an hour or some that are only about 10 minutes. Again, as long as you deliver the promised value, length should not be a concern.

STEP TWO: Create Your Lead Generation Website

Whichever website creator tool you decide to use,

or even if you decide to invest your own web presence and build a site on your own domain name, the most important thing is the capability for your webpage to collect leads.

An effective lead generation website should not contain a lot of content. Rather, there should be an eye-catching block of text that grabs the visitors' attention the moment they enter the site, and the copy should give them enough interest to continue reading.

You will then introduce to the visitors what free gift you are giving away. While the graphics and images do not need to be spectacular, they should be good enough so that the webpage as a whole can command the respect of a visiting prospect.

The visitors will then be presented with your free gift, as well as instructions on how to gain access. To do so, they would need to enter in their name and email address in your form.

STEP THREE: Follow Up With Emails

As with most traditional Internet marketers, your way of staying in touch with your prospects with this online system is through the use of emails. You will also use email marketing to continue building your relationship with the prospects.

With the plugin elements earlier described that will send you the content of the filled form, this is definitely cool technology. However, the downside is that if you are required to keep track of your leads and manually email them, there is no way your business will be automated.

This is where the use of automated email marketing software comes in. There are a selected few software on the market that are free, but any email marketing software worth mentioning will most likely require an investment.

If you believe that time is money, then your investment would certainly be worth it. With this automated email marketing technology, not only will the software quietly collect the leads into a database for you, but you can also set it to automatically send out emails at set intervals.

For example, the moment somebody signs up for the free report, video or whatever else, an introductory welcome message email instantly goes out to your prospect. The email can be customized to include whatever message you want, including a personal greeting, value-added content and a link to access the promised report or video.

After that, again at time intervals that you set, you can have the software send out additional email content for your new subscribers. This can include related articles, YouTube videos or other resources that are sent out each day, every week or whatever time interval you scheduled.

According to studies on email marketing, it takes about seven to ten emails for you to build a solid enough rapport with a new subscriber to finally be able to effectively send them an offer, which could be a product, service or business opportunity.

Following the same theory, you should plan to send a series of pure content emails for several days, then only introduce your business opportunity to them after you have legitimately built a trusting relationship with the subscriber.

Again, with this software, everything can be automated, so you do not have to worry about who signed up on which date, and which email to send to whom since they have already been in your database for several days and beyond.

STEP FOUR: Send Prospects To Your Salespage

After several emails, your prospects are now ready to view your offer, which should be presented to them in the form of a salesletter. As previously mentioned, this salesletter should ideally be anywhere between 15 to 20 pages, comprising again of an attention-grabbing title on top of the page.

The salescopy should then transition smoothly throughout the entire page, from the introduction of the letter and rapport building with your readers, all the way down to the final offer and investment. Through it all, as the prospect reads the salespage, social proof of testimonials and other success stories are also featured through text, images and videos.

Finally, at the end of the salesletter, state clearly what the prospect needs to do in order to sign up, and reveal the instructions step-by-step. You may want to include screenshot images of the signup process to make sure the prospect fully understands the steps to become your partner.

STEP FIVE: Send More Follow Up Emails

Even though many people may not sign up for your opportunity right away, the follow up process does not necessarily have to be manual. With the same email marketing technology, you can also automate this process.

After you send the message with the link to your salesletter, you can schedule your software to continue sending them more content. This way, it would not seem as if you are only going after them for the sale, and if they decide not to join, you would stop communicating with them.

If this is the perception that you give your prospects, your entire reputation is tarnished, and there is a good chance that they or anyone in their circle would never sign up with you. Word also spreads quickly in the social media world, and it is not uncommon for brands to get ruined quickly by negative online reviews.

To settle this matter, schedule in more content to send them. Give them more articles and videos on the topic, further building your rapport with them. Before anyone can learn to trust you, you must do your part by providing massive value.

After a while, send them the link to your salesletter again, followed by a message that asks them to reply to you if they have any questions. When you get around to it, also create the webinar videos and personal selling videos discussed in previous chapters, and send those to them, too.

The name of the game is to continue sending different ways of presenting the offer to them until they ultimately sign up, or they explicitly ask you never to contact them again. At which point, you can quietly unsubscribe them from your email database.

However, when all is said and done, following up with your prospects is a surefire way to get you more signups, regardless of whether the process was automated or not.

*****

There you have it, your five-step blueprint to build your own automated lead generation, follow up and sign up online system. The hardest part is setting up the actual system itself, but once it is done, all you need to do is what I mentioned to you in the beginning of this book: Generate leads.

All day and all night, whenever you have some spare time, spend a few minutes to promote your link. Post them to the masses by spreading the word in popular Facebook Groups and Pages, or simply invest a few dollars to send some targeted traffic your way effortlessly. Trust me, it will be money well spent.

CHAPTER CONTRIBUTION #1
■■

Multiple "Out Of Nowhere" New Partner Online Sign Ups From Someone Who Himself Is Also A Partner Who Signed Up Online From "Out Of Nowhere"

Contributor: Andrew Cheah
Protégé, Lead Mentor, Team Leader, Speaker, Trainer, Elite Coach

One of the key features that attracted me to this business is the automation system. As I am a person who values my time freedom, I want to work on a business that allows me to do more with less and also to expand my business easily.

From all my years of experience as an entrepreneur, I know that only businesses with good processes and systems are able to fulfill these 2 requirements.

Before I embarked on this online network business, I had set up my own online marketing systems in the past, and it took me months to set the whole thing up.

The funny thing is that even after I had set up everything, I still didn't generate any leads or received any prospects for a long time.

Furthermore, I had to write my own follow up emails to get my prospects or subscribers engaged, which is really not my cup of tea. Even just sending out a value-added informational email to my subscribers was not an easy thing for me due to my hectic schedule. After a while, I gave up.

To set up an effective online marketing automation system, it requires the following:

- Writing website copy
- Building the lead generation website
- Setting up the subscribers' email capturing system
- Creating your free report, ebook or gift
- Writing the follow up email series and
- Keeping your subscribers' engaged consistently

It took me easily more than 30 days to set all these things up. If this were your first time to do this, it would most likely take you more time because you still have to learn while doing it. If you have all the time in the world, then you can take your own sweet time to set it up, but I don't have the time.

On the other hand, I also had to spend quite a sum of money to set up this system for website domain, web hosting, and the emailing automation system. All these had easily costed me more than USD1000 annually.

Therefore, when I first read the salesletter from the Internet, I could not believe that this business actually comes with a complete online marketing automation system. It even includes a completed lead generation website with nice graphics, professionally written copy, lead capturing pages, Facebook templates, email automation and follow up system.

The great news is that they are all free for me to use. Not only that, but this partnership also gives me the right to allow my future business partners to use them.

What this means is that I can immediately start my business and make money on the spot. This is one of the best business-in-a-box packages that I have encountered in my life, and after observing so many before, I can also say it is the most affordable.

By the way, if you have doubts on whether the online system works or not, I can assure you that it really works because I am the living proof. You see, I joined the business from just reading through the lead generation website or salesletter.

That's right. Nobody called me, messaged me, talked to me, or contacted me in any way. Actually, I had never even met or conversed with my sponsor at all at that point. The salesletter copy is so convincing that I felt like I just had to grab this business opportunity right then and there, and I am glad that I have done that because my life never became the same again.

Because it worked on me, I truly believe in the automation system and I just followed the process of promoting. Amazingly, with the strategies that only took me minutes to learn and apply, I immediately started to generate leads of my own.

Even more amazing is that within only weeks after starting the business, I already had my own "out of nowhere" experience, as the system actually managed to help me get new business partners to sign up 100% online.

In the same way that I signed up online, these new partners joined under me without me even having to meet them face-to-face. I did not even have to talk to them or message them. It is as if they had come to me from thin air.

To me, this disruptive online marketing business has really changed my perception about the network marketing business and home business industry as a whole. The reason is, I simply hate the traditional face-to-face meetings.

However, just like everybody else who

understands it, I love the network marketing business compensation plan since it allows me to earn passive income. With this system, I can now take part in this lucrative business model previously reserved for the outspoken entrepreneurs, except every day, all I am doing is promoting this opportunity to complete strangers online with some very simple strategies that only takes minutes to apply.

Since young, I have been an introvert, so if you told my mum that I can make money from a network marketing business, she would be shocked. However, thanks to this disruptive marketing system, online marketing strategies and the selfless guidance from my mentors, I am now able to earn passive income from network marketing business.

CHAPTER CONTRIBUTION #2

Automation System Allows A Team Member To Implement Online Strategies To Generate International Leads Where New Partners From Multiple Countries Are Signed Up From "Out Of Nowhere" While On Holiday

Contributor: John Chuah
Team Leader, Speaker, Elite Member

The thing that attracted me to this business was the Internet marketing aspect. I saw the potential of the Internet towards any business, and in the back of my mind, I knew that if we can learn the skills to market our products or services online, the world would be our oyster.

Unfortunately, most of us are new to this. We have all heard about Internet marketing and online businesses, but we do not know anything about it. Where do we start? What do we need to do? Who do we turn to if we get stuck?

It seems like a lot of hurdles to begin with.

Luckily for me, I have my mentors who are already Internet gurus. So what I did was simply follow what our gurus has taught us in their training sessions.

I told myself, "They are the experts in this field, so why reinvent the wheel?"

Hence, I learned from them, one step at a time. Learn, apply, and test. Take the next step. Learn again, re-apply, do another test. Repeat until you get the hang of it.

Isn't that what we do in daily life? In our jobs?

Once I have gone through the trainings, I decided to start with Facebook Ads first as a way to promote the business. It was something I was comfortable with because I use Facebook all the time, and I see the ads every day.

Fortunately for me, shortly after joining the team, there was an immediate event coming up in Jakarta, Indonesia, so I could create my first FB ad to promote it. Although I had my reservations and doubts on the success of it, I decided to TAKE ACTION and promote it.

Like what Tony Robbins says "The path to SUCCESS is to take massive, determined ACTION."

It wasn't as hard as I thought it would be because of the training developed by the mentors. In fact, I easily created five ads to promote the event!

One important thing I have learned is that we need to monitor the "effectiveness" of the ads. If the ads are not delivering to the target audience, drop the ad. Like I said earlier - One step at a time. Learn again, re- apply, then do another test.

Eventually, out of five ads I created, one of them was performing very well! To my pleasant surprise, it actually registered interest for the preview!

Because the event was in another country, I couldn't find the time to go there. Despite this, the show went on with Simon Leung as the presenter, and with the help of the team who was there, they actually helped me to sign up my new partner!

To me, this new partner literally joined the business under me from "out-of-nowhere" because I had never met this person before, and I wasn't even there. Imagine if you can get new partners from other countries without you being there physically to attend the event! Can you imagine the potential if we do this well especially if we promote it globally?

So this proves that what our mentors taught us works, and combined with the online and offline systems that have been set up, they make it as automated for us as possible. My mentors have gone through the process, come out with a proven system, and we just have to follow it. Simple, isn't it?

Another method taught was how to use popular messenger apps like Whatsapp and WeChat to promote the events. One week after the Jakarta event, there was another event in my home city Kuala Lumpur, Malaysia.

Even though the event is in my own hometown, I would be traveling to Australia during that time and wouldn't be able to attend. Since I had to prepare for my trip and time was is short, I decided to give this method a try and used Whatsapp to promote the event.

With the process that was taught, I started sending out the preview link to my contacts. Again, I wasn't sure whether it would work because I couldn't make it to the event.

In my messages, I did not even need to explain in full detail the purpose of the event because the event link already has all the necessary information. It's completely done up for us. All we have to do was to promote it using some copy-and-paste script that was also written for us. It's that simple.

So can you imagine how surprised I was when I was informed that after Simon Leung presented again, I have yet another partner who joined the business under my team from "out-of-nowhere?" This was while I was in Australia, enjoying quality time spent with my family. My mentor, the team and systems in place pretty much did it all. It's AMAZING!

Within a few short weeks, I already had two partners who joined the business from "out-of-nowhere." Now, I will make time to work closer with the team so not only will I get more, but it would be great to contribute back to the team who has already given me so much.

Note that this is only one of the methods to promote this business via the Internet. I am now very eager to learn the other aspects of promoting this online from my mentors.

This is a simple business. We don't have to complicate it. Just follow the proven system and follow the guidance given by our mentors. Despite my short time doing this, I have already achieved some success, which is already beyond my own expectations, and I believe anyone can do it, too!

Let me end with a quote from Robin Sharma - "Dream BIG, Start small, ACT NOW!"

CHAPTER CONTRIBUTION #3
■■■

From Accepting A Free WeChat Session To Accepting Invitation To Live Mini-Seminar, Convinced Partner Signs Up On The Spot Before The Presentation Was Over Without Even Knowing Identity Of Sponsor

Contributor: Seow Wei Tang
Team Leader, Speaker, Elite Member

You have heard how some partners got into this business from out of nowhere. I am one of them.

I was actively seeking for new business opportunities. So I have been reading articles, watching videos on Internet marketing and attending previews for ideas on what to venture into.

That was when I came across a Facebook advertisement while browsing through my newsfeed that invited me to a free WeChat session on Internet marketing. The WeChat invitation promised to reveal some secrets about Internet marketing, so curiosity got the better of me and I registered for it.

The organizers did a very good job on this particular WeChat sharing session. It was informative, easy to understand, and it was like listening to a friend sharing his thoughts, so I found myself agreeing with the speaker's ideas.

At the end of the WeChat session, the speaker extended an invitation to a live preview session promising to share more valuable information. Because the free online session did such a great job building trust and rapport to the listeners, myself included, I naturally agreed to it in order to find out more.

At the live preview, I was reassured that something spectacularly was brewing by the presence of a large team. The ideas expounded earlier in the WeChat session were expanded even further here, and that reinforced my agreement with them.

I had several concerns about Internet marketing, like what products to sell, how to set up the platforms or automate the processes, and how to generate leads without burning a big hole in my pockets.

To my surprise, the team also identified the same issues as I did and offered solutions to each one of them. It was as if they read my mind. My confidence in this group went up several notches.

Halfway through their presentation of the business model, my mind was made up. I jumped off my seat with my hand raised asking to sign up. To their credit, they did not stop their presentation, but requested for me to please sit down and allow them to finish it.

Their package has everything I needed to succeed in this business; the step-by-step 6 weeks online training program, supplemented by live training sessions, lifetime leader mentorship, marketing platform and resources to simplify and track the leads, and lastly, the team support.

What about the lead generation? I wanted to know. "Don't worry, we will teach you," they reassured me.

From start to finish, from the point I responded to a Facebook advertisement, registered for a WeChat, participated in the WeChat, registered for the live preview, I did not have to interact, talk or chat with anybody.

In fact, my sponsor was not even on the WeChat session or the Live Preview, and I did not finally meet him until one month later. It is incredible when you think about it, that the entire process from beginning to end was fully automated to him.

So likewise, I know I can use this system and enroll prospects automatically without knowing and seeing them, literally "out of nowhere." This is amazing because it means that the system can be prospecting online and enrolling new prospects even when we may be busy with our other activities.

Having experienced the power of the live preview first hand, I was convinced that this has to be one of the key success features of the business. I was thus excited to get as many of my prospects to these live previews as fast as possible.

How did I approach my prospects?

Most of my prospects were approached as business partners. They had other concerns or grouses like job security, but when I was able to offer a viable solution, it built on my credibility and trust enough for them to register for the live previews.

Once they registered for the preview, I knew that there is a high chance of their conversion. This was eventually proven right as these prospects indeed registered on the spot after the preview.

Another partner was a classmate from another business course years ago which did not take off. As she was already of the business mindset, it was easy to discuss why this business model can work and why the other one failed.

Our discussion was purely done through an online chat. She accepted the invitation with an open mind and the live preview closed the deal for me. The wonderful part of the arrangement is that I can rely on the live preview to do all the talking for me, as I consider myself to be an introvert and typically shy away from business or sales presentations.

For this reason, my favorite way of getting prospects to the live previews was done mainly via online chatting. With this platform, I was able to reach out to a large group by posting short messages regularly and following up with them without needing to talk uncomfortably.

The advantage of this is that unlike a live conversation, I have time to craft my responses. As these chats can be done from a smartphone, I can work anytime and anywhere, assuming there is signal, that is.

To me, this is true freedom. Very seldom do I need to have a face-to-face meeting, but that should not pose a problem as any request to meet up creates an opportunity in itself.

Although other methods of prospecting may also be effective, live previews easily proved to have among the highest conversion rates and the sign ups tend to be more business-minded.

In order to maximize the success of the whole team, we need these business builders who attend seminars to grow the business. Therefore, live previews will always be my main weapon of choice, and with the teamwork of our members, even these events can result in "out of nowhere" partners.

With the proper training, the resources and team support, I have seen my business grow quickly, but as I continue to seed and sow, I also know that the best harvest has yet to come.

Here's to the team, who makes automation possible for newbies like myself, and make new partner sign ups possible whether we know them or not, and whether we are there or not.

CONCLUSION
Ready To Take Massive Action?
*****

Even though it may take a bit of time for newbies to digest everything we have discovered in this book, creating a profitable home business by building your network marketing business online is ultimately a pretty straightforward concept. You simply need to know what you are doing.

With over 10 years of professional experience as an Internet entrepreneur, I have seen enough online successes to know that this is a proven system that can be used to promote anything online. Yes, even network marketing products, services and the business opportunity itself.

Throughout my various network marketing projects in the past, and especially the one I am currently working on right now with my team, I am confident to say that I personally believe this unconventional hybrid system can work for anyone.

After all, with complete newbies with zero network marketing or online marketing experience actually able to leverage on our system to make sales from out of thin air and generate countless leads to plug into automated technology, it is safe to say that numbers and real results simply do not lie.

In this book, you have read about the details of our system, and now, you can take this information, replicate it and build your own if you want to Or, as Billy Teoh mentioned in the Foreword of this book, we welcome you to join us on our team with open arms, where the entire funnel system has already been created for you.

The online system itself is truly a work of art and when placed in the right hands, this masterpiece will make money for you and your team over and over again like clockwork.

Before I leave you, I want to make sure that you have gotten as much out of this book as you had intended. And if not, how can I help further? Do you want to personally connect with me and ask some questions? Or, would it help you to see our actual online system in action?

Since I have a knack of over-delivering (just ask my students and team members), I will provide you with both a way to get in touch with me, as well as the chance to witness our online sales funnel system in all its automated glory.

The link to access the said system, along with additional free valuable content, is in the "Resources" chapter of this book.

My website URL can be found in the "About The Author" section, but you are cordially invited to connect with me on my Facebook page, which you can access at Facebook.com/thesimonleung.

AFTERWORD BY JERRY CHEN WITH MICHAEL SINGLETON

"Putting It All Together: The Diamond Leader's Favorite Private Method To Personally Sponsoring, Motivating And Maintaining Over 2,800 Global Partners And Customers"

*****

Let's begin by letting the cat out of the bag. The secret private method is sales contests, otherwise known as incentives for team members. Why bother with incentives to motivate yourself and your team?

First and foremost, why should a leader consider creating an incentive program or contest(s)? If people are independent, shouldn't they be self-motivated and responsible for their own actions and success? Why should leaders invest their hard earned money and/or time initiating "silly" incentive programs or competitions to get people going? Certainly, if you are the type of leader who can influence growth within your team with your charm & charisma alone, then more power to you! Congratulations, no need to read any further! However, if you are like most of us, despite our best efforts, people do stall out, burn out & get frustrated over time.

To 'motivate' by definition means to provide someone with a motive for doing something or to stimulate someone's interest or enthusiasm for doing something. A huge mistake I have seen people make over the years is to act like a boss and treat their teammates like employees. This attitude is toxic in an environment like networking because being your own boss is often what attracts people to the industry in the first place! Making "boss like" statements or having "boss like" expectations may result in people quitting or harboring resentment towards you, and even the industry itself. Speaking to people in a condescending tone has caused more people to "exit stage left" than any product or business plan ever has!

You may be wondering, who is this guy? Has he always been perfect in this regard? Absolute and emphatic NO WAY! I have had many bad days and have definitely said things in a tone of voice that I have come to regret. I am sure I have lost people who I admire by saying the wrong thing in a harsh way. I have learned plenty through my own error and by observing others. To keep myself in check, I developed a mantra or phrase that I would utilize; "I never want to be the reason someone quits!" This mentality has had a negative impact as well. I have been called a "yes man" by some and perhaps have been perceived as passive and maybe even weak. I can live with that! My thinking is that it is better to error on the side of "taking the high road' than insisting on being right. Now, this does not apply when I or someone close to me is being disrespected. I will engage in conflict if the issue calls for it. My advice when it comes to conflict or difficult people is to choose your battles wisely. Weigh the risk.

If you find yourself in this industry long enough, chances are you too will have regret. Aiming for perfection is a sure way to fail. There are no perfect leaders. I propose that we just strive to treat people with dignity and respect as a general rule. How do you set yourself apart as a leader and not be a boss type? There is certainly an art to it, but incentives really help with motivating people in a positive way. They allow you to keep your team on a level playing field so that you don't inadvertently ignore anyone's achievements. Contest results will assist you as a mentor in identifying who may need more coaching an in what specific area.

In this current world we live in, it is my belief that incentives/recognition and competition are more important than ever to solidify a business team. Today, with information literally at our fingertips, product technology far superior than ever before, and a variety of marketing plans that have adopted the best parts of preexisting plans – there is no shortage of networking opportunities if someone is looking. The chance that we will come across someone open-minded is pretty high, as 51% of employed workers are actively seeking a new opportunity. In addition, people are quite well informed and it seems to me that long gone are the days people stay in one marriage or job for 40+ years, let alone their own business. Therefore, it is more important than ever to set your opportunity apart in creative ways in order to create team synergy, pride and most of all, loyalty.

Once you go through the process of getting a teammate in the door, your focus on them doesn't end; in fact, it is just beginning. The mission is not only to keep them in the door, but inspire them to want to bring others in as well! Sponsoring or recruiting incentives are terrific because once an individual adds members to their team; they now have more of a reason to stay involved. Another way to say it is, they now have something (or someone) to lose should they decide to leave! Not wanting to get left behind can be a catalyst to action for many people. They don't want to be left in the dust, especially by someone they shared the business with! Friendly competition among peers can be very positive.

What is to keep people from leaving for what they perceive in the moment as a better opportunity? In my opinion, the team culture, dynamic and emotional connection will be the glue that holds your team together. Retention can be a big issue in any business. We always need to be cognizant of the fact that human beings can get restless, bored and can be fickle, especially if they are in a temporary slump. We also have the generation gaps. Generation X'ers & Y's may respond to one type of incentive/ business model while millennial demand a completely different program. Baby Boomers are set to live longer than ever and may be focused on an entirely different experience that pertains to their stage of life! However, one thing that has universal appeal no matter the age differences is… FUN! People want to experience laughter. They need an escape from their daily grind. They want to be involved with a community that allows them to see the glass as "half full" instead of "half empty!" They long to have community & connection in this technology driven world. Your business team can become attractive to all ages & all walks of life, provided there is an element of joy, appreciation and success aligned with it.

When designing your contests, even if the reward has an educational component built in, add fun to the framework as well. If you make people laugh, and then in the same breath, they receive a zinger of knowledge, they are more likely to hear it, embrace it and remember the information.

Another reason to invest in your team with incentives or time is to increase revenue & volume. Incentives offer a way for individuals to track & record their work and receive recognition for their activity & results. Incentives can be the difference maker between performance and peak performance! It is doing that "one more thing" that can lead to victory. Tracking activity & results gives a sense of purpose and helps those who struggle with consistency to prevail. Stopping and starting is the kiss of death in this industry. Momentum is like magic and is what many teams lack. Having an objective through incentives allows for individuals to see how their own small daily victories can lead to personal achievements and also contribute to the team's overall goal. They sense that their achievement is part of something bigger. Don't underestimate the power of being part of the larger team and contributing to it. As individuals measure their own success and see how it directly affects the team goal, synergy begins to erupt.

In review, the main reasons why we would consider incentives are:

1. Increase retention/ loyalty
2. Increase revenue/ volume
3. Increase growth
4. Create team synergy & momentum through shared successes and goals
5. Friendly competition sparks activity

As you look forward, where do you begin? The first thing I believe is to define your objective. Be specific in what you would like to achieve and make sure your team is aware of the team goal. Because everyone coming on board is at a different ambition & skill level, it is up to each individual to declare their own goal. Some will choose to participate in incentives and others will sit back and watch. That is normal and ok. The leaders' intention is to assist those who are ready to accomplish what they set out to do.

Once you determine what you want to achieve as a team, set a budget for what you can and are willing to invest for a reward.

Finally, look at the make-up of your team members; their personalities, age range, etc... and attempt to choose a reward that will incentivize the most number of people or has aspects within the incentive that will appeal to a large number of them. The prize should reflect the level of activity & effort required as well as the accomplishment itself. If the goal is too easy & too many people achieve it, that translates that it isn't a distinct or special feat. If it is too difficult & not enough people achieve the goal, lack of belief can befall. The question of whether it is possible to succeed at all may infiltrate their minds and lead to a subsequent lack of action. It can be a balancing act, but often when bringing your team leaders in on the design itself, it comes out just right!

The total length of time of the incentive is also something to consider. Shorter incentives give a faster result and keep people's attention. Another perk is that the newest members can usually get on board, whereas longer incentives reward consistency, but the newest person may have to wait quite awhile to get in on the next one.

A combination of incentives is smart. I often opted for 90-day stretch goals that would go from one conference to the next. This worked quite well as people tended to get quite inspired leaving the event and the incentive helped keep them on task till the next event. I also recommend an annual incentive to reward loyalty, & consistency. These achievers are the core, the heart and soul of any business. The makeup of this group is not just the most outgoing & loudest of team members, but quite often, this group consists of the quiet yet strong loyal ones, slow but steady.

There are different types of incentives to consider. The main ones that come to mind are:

Physical/ Tangible Awards

A physical award can be anything from a certificate/trophy to fun awards. For example, it could be a stuffed animal that somehow represents the spirit of the team. Maybe a Lion signifying strength or a rhino signifying that nothing will stand in the way. Maybe the award is a statue of an Eagle representing leadership.

The award can be presented in a group setting, which gives the recipient something tangible, but also edifies them in front of their peers. The award can be something that is passed on from one person to the next, as each individual finds their own team members to share it with. The benefits of a physical award is that it can range in cost if the budget is tight and also, it is something that people will look at for years to come and remember their accomplishment.

Here are some examples:
- Trophy
- Certificate
- Theme Gift from an Event
- Symbolic Gift (Stuffed animal, figurine etc...)

Trips/ Vacations

If budget allows, trips can be a huge motivator. This is especially true if the trip has built in components of spending time with other "winners" or leaders within your organization. Rubbing elbows with successful people is hugely motivating as well as educational for them.

The trip can be something that individuals pay for on their own, but are not invited to unless they hit the incentive, or it can be something you choose to pay for yourself. Most importantly, take videos & photos to commemorate each event. This way, you can share it as a motivation for others to hit their own goals.

In my experience, some of the best reward trips had a team building aspect to them.

Here are some examples.

➢ House Boating: House boating trips are not necessarily inexpensive, but they are very effective in terms of building team cohesiveness. Over the years, I have hosted or joined many house boating adventures ranging from 5 to 30 houseboats. Most of the time, the trips were adult only and a few were with children. Both have different benefits, but are very different in the experience. The trips without children, we would have 3-4 couples or singles (around 8 people or so) on each boat to share expenses of meal planning & supplies. There were water sports, fishing, cooking together, movies on the top deck, round table discussions and strategy sessions throughout the trip. The most important feature was the fact that many of the attendees would have never had such an experience in their lives and perhaps haven't since then, and the memories shared united the team in a unique way. Overcoming things like wind or mice coming on board to sharing a bathroom & even injuries, while frustrating, can also bridge gaps and at the end of it, people couldn't wait for the next time! Trips with children provided families to build relationships as their children bond. Talent shows involving children are great for creating memories. I have been blown away over the talent of the individuals within my organization.

➢ Ropes / Challenge Coarse/ Teambuilding Weekend: I once hosted a Team Building Weekend in the mountains of Big Bear for all those who hit a certain volume level. It was a volume that was a stretch, but very attainable. The trip was the reward and the individuals paid for it themselves in order to be with the other high achievers. Throughout the weekend, there was a series of team building exercises, both physical and mental, that brought the team together in a very unique way. Corporations do these as well and they really can be powerful if done correctly. I hired a professional organization to handle the itinerary, but at each event, I would build in a gathering to recognize publicly each individual who attended. Highest achievers were given opportunity to speak/recognize their own team members. Always share the spotlight with the new class of emerging leaders & give them a taste of what it feels like to lead. Leadership doesn't happen overnight, it comes in the small defining moments and as a mentor, it is our responsibility to set people up to win by giving them opportunities to demonstrate their own style as a leader.

➢ Resort Destination Weekend: A luxury

weekend or week at a resort is something that many people will push themselves out of their comfort zones to achieve. A Hawaiian vacation or a weekend skiing, or to Palm Springs or Las Vegas. Anything associated with "status" success and class will get people excited. A mountain resort in Yosemite with music, food and nature hikes proved to be a lovely experience for attendees. There really is no limit when it comes to fantastic places to venture to.

➢ Cruise: A 3-day to a week-long cruise is a reward that many people will appreciate and set their sights on. The great thing about cruises is that everyone is basically in one place and runs into each other constantly, eats in a group, goes to shows and excursions together. Group rates can be a huge benefit and meals included are a plus, too. Cruises do tend to alienate a percentage of people who get sea sick, but I have found more often than not, those people tough it out so as not to miss anything!

➢ Extreme Sports & Activities: Over the years, I have had some serious adrenaline junkies within the ranks of leadership on my team. These people were wonderful because they were so different than me. Together, we could relate to more people. The secret not only to embrace these differences, but use them to the advantage of the team. I welcomed their initiative and requested they organize very special rewards for those who needed to get their heart pounding. And yes, I participated in some, but not all. Sometimes, I just went along to take photos and watch! Some examples are Bungee Jumping, Sky Diving, Rock Climbing, and Mechanical Bull Riding, to name a few. Some ideas that may be slightly more mild are horseback riding, ice/roller skating, mountain biking, hiking, sailing, etc... eat "Coal walking" types of experiences that cause us to get out of our comfort zones and face our fears together definitely caused tight bonds to form within a team. Adventure sports or activities can provide a lot of bang for the buck in terms of promotional video and filling up the memory banks.

➢ Dinner Cruise / Holiday Lights Cruise: A dinner cruise is another option where you can obtain group rates, keep people nearby and experience something beautiful.

Financial / Material Rewards

It was very rare that I personally offered financial rewards. In fact, in my experience, it was somewhat effective, but not as effective as other incentives. I once gave out $1,000 cash to people for hitting certain levels. I thought this would be a huge motivator, but at the end of the day, fewer people than expected actually completed the incentive, and even less were able to maintain the momentum after it was over. I am not really certain why this was my experience, but money alone didn't seem to keep people focused consistently. In addition, whatever rewards you personally offer, you want your team to believe that they too can one day do that. Duplication is powerful. By tossing out cash, duplication was lost in translation as most people have a difficult time seeing themselves in a position to do that. In addition, if money alone could do the trick, then a fantastic marketing plan should get people going consistently all on its own!

In conclusion, perhaps our efforts to motivate our teams should be in more creative ways that to just throw more money out as a solution. Often, the marketing plan/company you are partnered with will offer great material and financial rewards that you can promote. Tap into those rewards by building excitement around the company & things they offer/ if applicable!

➢ Cash
➢ Cars

- Motorcycles
- Trips
- Boats

Recognition Rewards

If I can share one secret to building a large organization/team, it would be this: Edify, recognize, praise, thank & love your teammates, mentors, friends & associates. But especially pay attention to your team and their accomplishments. Recognition rewards have been one of the single most powerful weapons in my arsenal over the years, as well as the most personally satisfying. Most of us desire to be recognized for our achievements and praised for a job well done. There are so many ways to recognize the efforts of individuals. Utilizing social media, text messaging or e-mail are cost effective, can reach a lot of people and is easy to do.

At seminars, conferences and events, a special ribbon, button, bracelet, shirt, hat, etc. to set people apart can be used. (Know your team and if they will perceive this as a positive thing.)

Edification in front of one's peers is truly motivating for most. To be singled out and noticed for your efforts is encouraging to the individual and also to those who witness it.

Intimate discussions whereby you just thank a person for their confidence and trust and for choosing to partner with you can also be important. Thank people often and sincerely for their contribution or just their presence and encouragement! There is no such thing as doing this too often or too much.

Note of Caution: You will undoubtedly prefer working with certain people over others. Some people are high maintenance, while others are a pure joy. Some people take your energy while others give you energy. However, as a leader, it is imperative that you do your absolute best to recognize achievements as equally and as fairly as possible within your group. This is where official incentives really help take the guesswork out of who to pay attention to. It may seem like a non-issue when just starting out, but when your business grows from 10 people to 1000 people, it can become daunting. It is super easy to leave people out when lavishing on the praise! Having spelled out incentives for people to hit helps leaders to remain objective when they recognize achievements and prevents over inflating one person's ego at the expense of someone else.

Some examples of recognition rewards are:

➢ Name/photo in print for others to see listing

accomplishment. (Facebook, Twitter, Instagram, E-mail, Newsletter, on screen at an event, etc.)

➢ Stage time: Stage time at an event to tell their own story, share their history and goals, even if only 3 minutes really inspires people. Not every leader has the ability to do this, due to proximity, not being in charge of the event, etc. But, if you have the ability to give people a "voice," it can be a powerful motivator. Another option would be to interview them on a team conference call. They will feel respected and can share what they have learned so far. Win win!

➢ Phone Calls or Face Time with their Leader: If you are their mentor, take them out to coffee or lunch. Give them your quality time and focus to help those set goals, answer questions, and listen to their dreams. If they have another mentor that seems untouchable, but you have access, ask this leader to send them a message via social media or telephone. Hearing from someone that they respect in the industry is very encouraging and just takes the leadership a little bit of time.

➢ Special event or party that recognizes a specific achievement.

➢ If you attend a trip or vacation, send post cards to team members not only to encourage them, but to also let them know that you recognize you didn't get there alone – and they will get their turn as well!

As a side note, have the attitude that you are there for your team. Your mission is to serve them, help them, inspire and reward them! When leaders start to see their team as being there to serve their own personal agenda, they can get lost. Their team feels this disconnect and the leader fails to endear themselves to the team. Also, if you ever come to a cross roads or are having difficulty with a decision, when in doubt, always do the thing that is best for the team member, not you. Yes, even if this comes at a financial loss for you. You will sleep better knowing that you didn't take advantage of anyone. In fact, just the opposite will be true. You will be trusted and have their devotion, which in this industry is far more valuable than money!

The longer you are involved in this industry, you will see people come in to your business life and out of your business life. Sometimes they return, other times they don't. It isn't easy. When we invest time, resources, money and most of all belief in people, it can be not only frustrating when they move on down the road, but it can be painful, too. We must develop thick skin when it comes to this issue. Never leave a negative wake by calling someone a quitter or other derogatory term. Always, leave the door open for them to return if and when they are ready. Remember, they don't owe you anything. Like the stock market, you invested in them knowing there may not be a return, and it is the risk we take. Investing in people is never a waste. There is always good that comes from it, even if we are not the direct recipients of that good. The ones that leave may become better parents or friends, save more money, get out of debt, get promotions at work, grow their self confidence, etc. There are sometimes invisible growth that occurs, and we just need to have faith that it is worth it. There will also be people that come into your life that are such low maintenance, they are like a dream. They will balance out the scales, I promise you.

When we adopt the philosophy that we are here to serve people for wherever they are in their personal journey, knowing some will be in for the long haul, others just a pit stop, it helps just a little with the pain of loss because it isn't about you as their leader, it is about them and their own goals, dreams and aspirations. The way of life of a networking professional is not for everyone! With great success comes the struggles of dealing with a few difficult people, but that's not different than anything in life. The amazing people you will meet that you otherwise would never know will enrich your life in incredible ways! The sooner we recognize this fact, the more we can enjoy the process, wherever it leads. Love everyone, depend on no one.

Association Rewards

This is listed last because association rewards can be incorporated into trips & physical rewards & event pre-existing seminars or conferences. In fact, any time you can link group association into anything you do, the stronger a team you will have. There is something magical when like-minded individuals come together for a common objective combined with being included in an elite group of people.

Here are some examples.

At a conference (if you are running it or just an attendee), you can pull your incentive winners aside for a special training or time at the conclusion of the main event. I have done:

➢ Ice Crème Socials.
➢ Advanced Training after the main meeting.
➢ Party in my Hotel Suite or banquet rooms with just soda & snacks.
➢ Visit at the party from a higher level mentor/leader to give an inspiring speech.
➢ Gift basket in their hotel room from me with

snacks for the weekend. (products from our business if appropriate) OR a special gift sent to their room.

➢ Decorate the high achievers hotel room.

➢ Special invitation to leaders home for a dinner banquet, meeting or party. I had many dinner banquets & pool parties at my home.

Incentives can be short term for 30 days as an example, whereby the team tracks their progress and at the end of the 30 days, they hit it or not. Short-term goals are terrific because they are quick and people don't lose focus as easily, therefore leading to more success. I have always preferred the idea of tracking not only results, but activity. Activity can be controlled, allowing a person a win. Results can vary depending on the how effective the person is. Incentives that measure both are great also.

Incentives based on activity can track action and personal growth activities. Perhaps you can create a tracking sheet on line, paper or even a computer app or spreadsheet that can track daily goals met.

Daily Goals (assign a point value to each activity and at the end of 30 days whoever achieves a certain number win the reward). More difficult tasks should get more points. Easier tasks get less. Choose a target number based on a combination of easy and more difficult tasks.

➢ Read 10 pages minimum in a business enhancing book.

➢ Listen to something positive (audio book, pod cast, motivational speaker, etc.)

➢ Add one new person to your contact list, Facebook, Instagram, etc. (Meet someone new who can lead you to someone new.)

➢ Text/ Call / E-mail your mentor to report in what you accomplished that day. (Accountability)

➢ Reach out to team members to provide encouragement and help if needed.

➢ Learn something new about your product(s) or share what you learned with your teammates on a team website, blog, Facebook or whatever is appropriate.

➢ Share your product with someone new.

➢ Establish a new client/customer. (Autoship if applicable or initial order).

➢ Follow up with past client(s)/customer(s).

➢ Promote your business to a new person. Share the business plan.

➢ Add new team member! Recruit/Sponsor.

➢ Participate in a conference call training.

➢ Attend a meeting / event in person.

➢ Hit a new level in the marketing plan.

These are just a few ideas. You can customize your daily tracking to your own business venture with your own business language.

I have had great success with year-long incentives as well, but these are best when there is an element of control associated with it. A controlled action, as an example, is how many people you share your business with. An uncontrolled result is how many actually get started.

For example, I ran 12 for 12 Volume incentives. Volume is somewhat easier to control than sponsoring new businesses, so a yearly incentive works well with volume as opposed to new business. The product line that I worked with had a variety of consumables available. The yearly incentive was to achieve a personal volume goal of 300 points, which was equivalent to somewhere between $600 - $800, depending on the product. We had a slogan use 100 pts, eat 100 pts and sell 100 pts. Of course, there were always some families with 4 children that maybe ate or used more, and some single people that had to focus on selling more, but the incentive was the same for everyone. At the end of the 12 months, all of those who achieved the goal were part of the Special Club and invited to an awards banquet in their honor. The theme for the event was different each year, which added to the excitement. Here are some examples of some of the theme events that were done. People really stretched to hit this goal year after year. The parties were indeed special, but more than that they wanted to be part of the Club!

New business growth incentives (i.e. sponsoring, recruiting, etc.) work great with 30 – 90 day incentives because it is a skill that gets better and better with time. Having the ability to begin again in a month or 3 months keeps people from losing heart if they struggle in this area.

➢ Emerald City (a Wizard of Oz) event: Leaders within the team dressed in costume and performed a funny skit. The trophy or award was a Wizard of Oz snow globe, engraved.

➢ Masquerade Ball: On board the old luxury yacht, the Queen Mary, decorated with Candelabras and old fashioned décor. Achievers had the option of coming in 18th century costume. Upon entering their photo was taken and they were given a handmade Venetian style mask. A gourmet meal was enjoyed at award winning Sir Winston's Restaurant aboard the Queen Mary. Some spent the night on board the ship. It was a fun celebration and most had never been to anything like it!

➢ Pirates: Need I say more? People came decked out in Pirate garb, spoke like pirates and received pirate booty!

➢ Roaring 20's: Costumes were gangsters and flappers! Held at the Jazz Kitchen at Downtown Disney. A crystal saxophone was the trophy, live jazz music and flaming bananas foster for dessert! Great photos and video memories.

➢ Wild West: Everyone came in cowboy/cowgirl attire to the Saddle Ranch Chop House in Universal City Walk. Delicious dinner was served, huge portions. A lit up crystal block; with a laser etched bull rider was presented as the trophy. Mechanical bull riding competition followed.

This is just a small sampling of different themed events my organization has done. We have had many, many more over the years. (Fiesta, California Dreaming, Celebrity (come as a famous person), Biker Bash (Harley Davidson Themed), Safari, La Dolce Vita, (the good life - Italian theme on Venetian Gondolas and Italian food), World Travel (overlooking LAX airport, each table was a different country), Business is Blooming (garden theme), You are the Magic (professional magician), Super bowl, potlucks, Oscar them with paparazzi and red carpet, casino, luau, karaoke, black tie, 50's, 70's, 80's, sports, etc.

One of the advantages of themed events is that they give people a specific memory to associate to their achievement that a typical hotel chicken dinner banquet may not provide. The themed "trophy" or memento can go in a place of honor in their homes and they can relive that memory often. Also, more people got into costume than didn't as each year went by because more and more they didn't want to be left out! Other business teams often envied the special attention and celebrations I would attempt to shower on to my team. Nothing was too much or too over the top, and I was paid back 10 fold with loyalty, respect and most of all friendship!

The personalities of every team are different. What drives or motivates them as individual groups may be different as well. Often, it seems that a team is a reflection of their leader. Like-minded people attract people of like minds! Take a hard look at the individuals around you, discern what might "light them up," drive them, excite them and gear your incentives around those emotions.

The bottom line is that as a leader, you don't sit idle, expecting other people to just get inspired and stay inspired all on their own. If they do, count yourself lucky! The benefit of creating an environment that is rich in reward, association and accolades and most of all, is worlds away from the "business as usual" rat race will set in motion a contagious growth within your business. The camaraderie, duplication, team spirit, memories and fun will be a force to be reckoned with. When presented with a competitor's business model that is "just like yours only better," they will stay with you because they know that what they have far surpasses any amount of money or product line. Yes, it may have a terrific bonus structure and cutting edge products, but at the risk of sounding sappy, a family has been created, one where people can be the best version of themselves and it doesn't go unnoticed. In this family, people face their fears and overcome obstacles together. They share in the victories and hold each other up in the defeats. They can venture out of their box with no judgment if they need to hop back in for a bit.

Flip Side/Recognition and Appreciation for Your Mentors

One of the best ways to promote edification and appreciation throughout an organization is to be the best example of it yourself. Perhaps you are the one who has accomplished an incentive or goal. A suggestion would be for you to honor in some way those that helped you get there. Perhaps you present a single rose to the women who have helped you along the way. I once presented my mentors with a bronze horse statue because their home was in the Southwest style and they had horses. They loved it and it remains in their living room. Personalized gifts are very special. If you take the time to special order something with their name on it or that is sentimental or significant to only them, it will show that you put a lot of thought into it. Be thoughtful in honoring and appreciating those who have been there for you and your team, and they will treat you the exact same way!

If a business leader/mentor come into town or to an event as a special guest speaker, make an effort to really amp up the respect. Designate someone to act as their host, picking them up from the airport or making sure they have everything they need during their stay. Have the team get involved with putting gifts in their room (nothing expensive, they can bake cookies or have everyone sign a card of appreciation) to some these methods may seem "old school" or perhaps a waste of time. My belief is that any way that you can create an aura or shine a light upon achievement in your industry will only cause people to aspire to become a leader themselves.

Does it all work? Absolutely. At least for me, as at

the time of this writing, I have personally sponsored over 2,800 partners and customers all around the world, with the highest personal volume per distributor within the entire system/team.

Even though it may take a bit of time for newbies to digest everything we have discovered in this book, creating a profitable home business by building your network marketing business online is ultimately a pretty straightforward concept. You simply need to know what you are doing.

For additional help, definitely check out the resources page available in the next chapter. I personally look forward to connecting with you and hearing about your successes from this book!

Jerry Chen with Michael Singleton
Network Marketing Diamond Leaders

RESOURCES

*****

We intend to update our resources section often in order to provide you with all the latest and most up-to-date value. As such, please connect with us on our official Facebook Page and feel free to interact or contact any of our book contributors whom you will find on that page. There, you will find additional free gifts, live demos of our actual highly converting sales funnels, as well as more surprise bonuses that will continue to be added over time. Be sure to "Like" our page in order to follow us.

OFFICIAL FACEBOOK PAGE

Facebook.com/HomeBusinessBook

WHAT MORE TEAM MEMBERS SAY ABOUT THE STRATEGIES OUTLINED IN THIS BOOK

*****

"It's amazing for a complete newbie like me, who doesn't have any IT knowledge and no background in doing any sales in the past, to start an online business from home. I am so grateful to my mentor, Simon Leung, for his mentorship to transform me from a complete beginner into Internet Marketer that enabled me to earn passive income. For the first time in my life, I grew my Internet income from zero to four figures a month after learning the practical methods from Simon. I strongly believe that through Simon and his unbeatable Internet Marketing system and strategies, everyone can earn monthly 5-figures income and achieve freedom." – Jessica Jong

"I am a professional IT guy and an experienced and knowledgeable Internet marketer and network marketer for many years. All the while, I have been looking for a complete turnkey system and solution that can fully be implemented by Internet marketing strategies to do the network marketing business. When I did my research online, I found Simon Leung and his powerful lead generation strategies with mini courses to 'seduce' me step by step with free gifts, bonuses and materials until I just can't control and signed up the highest level package straight away without thinking twice. I knew this is my best choice so far and I definitely will put my effort 100% full force and will be successful very soon with the guidance of Simon Leung, Team Leaders and members. See you all at the TOP!" – Clarence Chew

"Network marketing is never for an introvert and a stay-at-home-mom like me. But with the free training and online business tools provided, it is no longer conventional network marketing anymore as it has now becoming an Internet marketing business. This makes us stand out from the rest that are doing the business purely the traditional way. Now, everyone can enjoy the lucrative network marketing income without doing network marketing." – Danyelle Tan Chiaw Lian

"Learning with Simon Leung and his Protégés is just an extraordinary experience and opportunity that was able to pull me up to another level as a network marketer. I've never thought network marketing can do it in such an incredible way and how powerful it is when combining it with Internet marketing." – Joshua Koay

"It's such a privilege to have Simon Leung and his Protégés as my mentors. They have supported and helped me to develop on many skills that are valuable in running a business. With their mentorship, I believe that everyone can be successful in business." – Janice Tan

"Never in my life would I have thought that I'd end up in network marketing. But with this amazing online platform, I'm much more confident to do my ecommerce business under the great mentorship of Simon Leung and his team. I'm so grateful that this online platform has helped me, a full-time working mom, to create a money making machine to provide for my family." – Jasmine Tang Li Yen

"My boy was diagnosed with congenital heart disease at birth, so I had no choice but to stay at home to take care of him after my delivery instead of going back to work. With his open-heart surgery, daily medicine and routine follow ups with the pediatric cardiologist, our medical fees surpassed 60,000. I was lucky to come across a post from a Facebook group about creating passive income with an online marketing business. After receiving all my support, training and coaching from my home sweet home, I took action and saw the power of the automated sales system! This is my "insurance" for my boy, all the while grateful for my mentors and business partners who are willing to share their secret weapons and experience. I'm a nobody now, but who knows, maybe I will be a somebody in the future. Thank you!" – Yap Hooi Ling

"Thank you to Simon Leung and his Protégé team for their leadership. I see a bright future in network marketing by leveraging on Internet marketing. All I have to do is be open-mind, coachable, and follow my leaders' teachings. I love this system so much and am willing to share to the whole world how this system can help everyone." – Dylan Goh Tse Liang

ABOUT THE AUTHOR

*****

Simon Leung is a world-renowned Internet entrepreneur, award-winning motivational keynote speaker, International best-selling author, global online marketing trainer, consultant, coach and mentor.

Born in Hong Kong, Simon grew up in San Francisco, CA (USA), where he, upon university graduation in 2001, attained close to five years of corporate experience as the most Senior Google Optimization Specialist at Google Headquarters in the Silicon Valley.

Since 2004, Simon has been marketing online, finally transitioning from a full-time employee into a solo Internet entrepreneur in 2006. Ever since then, Simon has traveled the world to share his expertise to countless students, often speaking across 16 countries a year and hundreds of cities.

Today, Simon still continues his personal online projects, global seminars and training courses, but has been limiting his public appearances so he can focus more of his time leading his online home business partners towards success and achieving their own lifestyle goals.

For more information about Simon Leung, learn more from him with his online video trainings or find out how to contact or hire him, you can directly connect with him on his website, which also contains links to his social media profiles.

WWW.SIMONLEUNG.COM

MEET THE CONTRIBUTORS

*****

Ming Liang is an Internet entrepreneur and online marketing consultant, and stay-at-home mom who operates her entire business from the comfort of her own home or during vacation travels. She is experienced in helping local businesses promote their brands and increase their sales volume through the World Wide Web. To continue chasing her own dream of helping others through changing people's lives, Ming Liang is frequently featured on the world's stages to share her own experience, story and knowledge to inspire those who deserve a change, especially for other stay-at-home moms like her who want to spend more time with their family.

William Cheong is an Internet Entrepreneur who inspired people across the world with his story of making USD1000 in one day from one hour of work when he started his Internet marketing journey towards the end of 2014. Today, he is a platform speaker, International coach, and marketing trainer.

Andrew Cheah is an entrepreneur and a supply chain consultant since 2000. He has spoken in more than 30+ countries and is known to be able to help corporations achieve fast results. On a personal level, Andrew loves coaching new entrepreneurs to excel in their businesses. Currently, his mission is to develop more entrepreneurs to make this world a better place.

Vincent Hoo was a licensed aircraft engineer for over two decades before finding a better way to make a living through the Internet. Vincent is just an ordinary guy, but his greatest win was how he created his journey of changing people's lives by leveraging on his own Internet marketing skills to build a global online business. Vincent achieved various successes under direct guidance and support from his mentor, Simon Leung, and earned the honor of following his mentor to seminars, where he provided trainings and shared his own experiences, all the while with the goal to create more success stories worldwide.

Elaine Pang is a qualified accountant by qualification. Since 1997, she runs her own consultancy firm providing accounting software setup, training and support services for small to medium sized businesses. After 12 years as a corporate accountant, Elaine decided to embark on being her own boss, becoming quite Internet savvy for someone her age. She learned to leverage on the Internet, specifically a business website, to generate inquiries and sales for her firm. Elaine now uses her newfound skills to generate passive income through building multiple Internet businesses.

Joshua Koay came from the background of computing and music. Other than being a musician, sound engineer and a trainer, Joshua is also an Internet entrepreneur beginning from early 2016. Joshua started his Internet entrepreneurship journey with zero experience, but was be able to create his own success story within a short period of time. This was done with his capability to create and set up his projects on the Internet and started to generate income within only a matter of 3 weeks. Today, Joshua continues to do what he does best on the Internet, and at the same time, he teaches and inspires people to achieve their dreams and goals of generating online income.

Pudji Sugianto is an IT professional who has been working in numerous IT companies in Jakarta, Indonesia. His interest in Internet Marketing lead him to get involved with a group of Internet entrepreneurs, and he is a member of an Elite Team led by world-renowned Internet Marketing guru, Simon Leung.

Jian Ming is the Founder and marketing consultant of Acelogy, a company that serves small medium businesses (SME). He is involved in NGOs like WorldVision and Befrienders. Jian Ming is also a certified NLP Practitioner, certified Business Success Coach, SAP® Certified Associate and Project Management Professional (PMP ®). An MBA holder, Jian Ming is currently pursuing his Doctorate in Business Administration. He strongly believes in contributing back to society and helping others succeed.

Dr. Fazley Rahman is a medical doctor and lecturer by profession. He has a great passion in teaching, public speaking, Internet marketing & e-commerce. As an Oxford University graduate, Dr. Fazley likes to think outside the box and set a good example for others to follow. He has attended many seminars by world-class mentors like Robert Kiyosaki, JT Foxx and Simon Leung. Dr. Fazley strongly believes that Internet marketing and e-commerce are the way forward. Currently, Dr. Fazley is on a mission to achieve financial freedom by helping as many people as possible.

Sam Eng is an Internet entrepreneur who actively conducts online business talks via WeChat and offline seminars. His 20+ years of corporate experience in marketing management and leadership has equipped him with all the valuable knowledge and experience that earn the appreciation of his loyal followers. Sam is also an MBA postgraduate from Nottingham Trent University.

Hendry Lee is a businessman of integrity and vision. He is also a professional forex trader who runs his own private funds manager. Nowadays, Hendry is inspiring and helping entrepreneurs to build and leverage their businesses through Internet technology. The concept behind Hendry's transformation is simple, as he believes this technology has changed the traditional way most people run businesses, and the new online way is the path to the future.

Danyelle Tan is a former project architect, and the Founder and Managing Editor of her own company.

Currently, she is a stay at home mom earning USD in her global ecommerce business. To inspire more ladies in their entrepreneurship journey, Danyelle is partnering with a group of Internet entrepreneurs and marketing experts to help open up learning opportunities and potential partnerships to more people around the world.

Nik Fuaad is a civil engineer by profession with more than 30 years of experience working with contractors, developers and consultants around the world. Having financial freedom at the expense of personal time freedom has prompted him to look for an alternative career as retirement looms. Now, Nik is committed to the Internet business as his last professional challenge to keep his youth adrenalin flowing.

Sok Kiang is a passionate tutor who works from home. She has a flair for building friendships with people from all walks of life and people tend to gravitate to her wherever she goes. Sok Kiang made the choice of working from home in order to help her son with special needs, and to cope with the daily challenges of life. As such, the Internet marketing business model serves her well as she now has the flexibility to manage the two roles and generate a tidy source of income from home.

Janice Tan is a young entrepreneur with a professional accounting qualification who is currently pursuing her Masters Degree in the University of London. She started her entrepreneur journey when she was still an undergraduate student back in 2015 and has created her own success story. Janice is now involved in both traditional and online businesses in different industries. Today, she is on a mission to inspire more people, especially the young adults like her, to pursue their entrepreneurial dreams.

Sungkono Surya Tjahyono is an entrepreneur from Indonesia. He graduated from the University of Auckland and pursued a dream career in the game industry as a programmer in Wellington, New Zealand. Surya's exposure to the IT world has inspired him to formulate a business blueprint in the creative industry to leverage on technology to help people financially. Nowadays, he spends most of his time building networks and connecting with people to inspire and realize his dream of helping underprivileged children in Indonesia.

Sue Tan is an Internet marketer by profession with a strong branding background and has been working in both B2C and B2B's multi-national companies. Sue was in the event management industry before she pursued her career in Internet marketing. As a Digital Marketing Specialist who started with zero experience, Sue picked up the knowledge along the way through training via online and offline. Sue believes in continuous learning, discovering new things, and growing.

Jasmine Tang is an Internet entrepreneur and a qualified educator by profession who is passionate in teaching to mold young generations to face the challenging society. Graduated from University Science Malaysia, she has achieved first-class honors in Bachelor of Science with Education. She is a young mom, juggling between family and work. As such, she ventures into Internet marketing to boost her income with much flexibility of time. With the strategies acquired in Facebook marketing courses, she is now building her online business simply with Facebook.

John Chuah has been in banking industry for as long as he can remember. Although he is established in his career, he soon came to the realization that all income will cease when one retires. After doing some research, John discovered that Internet marketing is an alternative solution of generating income. John attended a few

Internet marketing courses and has benefitted from them, but has finally found his true calling in Internet marketing, ecommerce, and online business. John is currently pursuing vigorously to achieve financial freedom for himself and his family.

Seow Wei Tang is a business consultant with more than 35 years of corporate experience. He is a turnaround specialist who has helped transformed struggling projects into profitable multi-million dollar businesses. With his training for spotting opportunities, Seow was able to quickly appreciate the power of online marketing and is currently being mentored by world-renowned Internet guru, Simon Leung. Seow also teaches at a local private university to share his love of knowledge with the younger generation, along with working on his Internet business to achieve personal freedom for himself and for others.

SIMON LEUNG
WWW.SIMONLEUNG.COM
FACEBOOK.COM/THESIMONLEUNG
FACEBOOK.COM/HOMEBUSINESSBOOK

www.ingramcontent.com/pod-product-compliance
Lightning Source LLC
Chambersburg PA
CBHW020856180526
45163CB00007B/2520